TEACH YOURSELF
CORRECT
MANNERS
and
ETIQUETTE

TEACH YOURSELF
CORRECT
MANNERS AND
ETIQUETTE

ERIC WATSON

HIND POCKET BOOKS

TEACH YOURSELF
CORRECT MANNERS AND ETIQUETTE

© All rights reserved, Hind Pocket Books, 1979
First Edition: 2002
First Reprint: February 2003
Second Reprint: March 2003
Third Reprint: December 2003
Fourth Reprint: January 2006
Fifth Reprint: September 2006
Sixth Reprint: November 2006
Seventh Reprint: June 2007
Eighth Reprint: February 2009

ISBN 81-216-0034-9

Published by
Hind Pocket Books Pvt. Ltd.
J-40, Jorbagh Lane, New Delhi-110003
Tel: 24620063, 24621011 • Fax: 24645795
Post Box No. 3005, Lodhi Road Post Office, New Delhi-110003
E-mail: fullcircle@vsnl.com • *website:* www.atfullcircle.com

Typesetting: SCANSET
J-40, Jorbagh Lane, New Delhi-110003
Tel: 24620063, 24621011 • Fax: 24645795

Printed at Dot Security Press Pvt. Ltd., Delhi-110028

PRINTED IN INDIA

02/09/09/02/11/SCANSET/SAP/DSP/DSP

CONTENTS

Introduction

*T*he day man left his abode in the jungle and proceeded to give himself a civilisation to improve and lift himself to higher levels of achievement was the point when social contacts began to have a special significance for him. Since then in all his dealings with his fellow human beings he has been presenting himself in an agreeable manner to get his ideas and objectives sanctioned through negotiations and persuasion instead of application of brute force. The family, the clan, the tribe, the village, all started to fortify themselves with sets of rules and regulations that were to distinguish each group, on the one hand and encourage discipline among the different individuals and members, on the other.

Starting with the family, where the head of the family has to see to the needs of those under him in return for gratuitous assistance and loyalty to the nation that came to be founded at a later period, every kind of social and human institution should be in a position to propagate the feeling of unity, belonging and cooperation among its component units. Customs, conventions and traditions and similar usages cropped up from time to time to render support to one institution of this nature or another. These traditions were generally forged out of the tried and tested actions and behaviours of human beings against the background of different types of social life. Our ancestors, who knew best and had the experience, already laid down the lines of action for posterity. True, there have been protests from the new generation now and then but ultimately these have petered out in the face of the inherent wisdom of established ways.

Evolution

Etiquette has evolved from all these loose ends of human actions and reactions in bilateral or multilateral relationships. Whenever and wherever two people meet, whether for business or for a friendly chat, whether to exchange words between relatives, acquaintances or strangers, there are some manners that automatically become discarded or relevant; and the science of etiquette has grown out of this relevancy. We do not question why and how a new bride has to behave in the manner she does among her in-laws, how a subordinate should behave towards his boss, how the guardian or the preceptor should behave towards his wards, how friends and colleagues or, for that matter, foes should ventilate their feelings for one another. If there is etiquette among nations appropriate to times of peace, there is also etiquette of war, with its code of conduct under which children, women, the wounded and those who have surrendered should be taken into custody and protected by the enemy, how the Red Cross code is not to be violated, and with what respect the white flag is to be treated in the face of conflict.

It is apparent that etiquette rules every field. The cultivated and cultured man many stop the multitude that was ready to defy the guns. Good behaviour makes its mark everywhere and is the key-note of social success. Courtesy costs nothing and is indeed priceless. The rude, the roguish, the wicked never truly make a headway, though they may boast of imaginary victories. Bad manners cannot be equated with strength. The firmness of the polite and the soft-spoken could be much stronger and more effective than the roughness of the toughest bully. Etiquette is concerned with a man's behaviour, it is not related to his gains or losses. A man may uphold the best of manners while making a profit, at the same time, he may not forget his gentlemanly ways while losing in the deal. This does not preclude, however, the need for being strong with the adamant, competitive with the aggressive, and gentle with the meek and the kindly.

Necessity

There are things that can be done in any way while there are others which are rated best in their respective fields. The difference between the former and the latter is that, in the competitive world, there is in the last analysis, scope and place for only the best, and actions that do not come up to the highest point of efficiency run the risk of getting discarded or dispensed with at some point of time. To avoid this pitfall, this uncertainty, it is obligatory on a person, who is charged with some duty that is to be fulfilled, to act in a manner which will leave no doubt about its acceptance. A shopkeeper may sell a thing which the buyer urgently needs and which, as is known to both the buyer and the seller, is not easily available, and yet if this shopkeeper clothes his product with suitable goodwill and ingratiating manners, he may bind this customer to him not only for that particular transaction but also for all types of possible purchases from his shop in the future.

The question of behaviour comes in more useful in an office where cooperation and competition exist side by side. An office worker may be very efficient in his work, be it typing, accounts, correspondence, selling or purchasing. However, if he cannot get along with people around him, it is doubtful whether he will go very far in his vocation. Consequently, though he may retain his seat in the office, he may scarcely make outstanding advancement, and since his juniors may surpass him in one way or another, it is possible that his temper or disposition will become more and more sensitive, and his work suffer and deteriorate in quality in the end.

In the same manner a business house cannot afford to be high and mighty in its dealings even though it may cater to exclusive groups of customers. On the other hand, the etiquette of keeping out the unwanted without being offensive may lie in the establishment's form, facade and glamour to such an extent that common people and ordinary customers will have a feeling of awe in approaching or dealing with such an establishment. The exceptions or the negligible few who overcome this mental fright presented by the grandiose front and framework of the establishment and venture inside should be treated gently and deferentially and by no means harshly.

Efficiency and etiquette do not over-lap nor are they mutually exclusive. From the aforementioned examples it is clear that they are gifts or acquirements which do not automatically co-exist. There may be efficiency without etiquette and etiquette without efficiency. That action is perfect and most fruitful where there is a happy blend of the two. Efficiency performs, etiquette establishes. Each of these is to be supplemented by the other to produce a good lasting effect. Etiquette is a necessity for a person who is efficient because that alone could assure his success and improve his periphery forever. For those who are not so efficient, etiquette might cushion their falls or failures, and their humbleness and popularity may make it possible for them to learn these things more quickly if they have the aptitude and the industry.

Lack of Etiquette

It is debatable whether lack of etiquette is a lapse or not. There may be persons of an extremely polite disposition who are used to good behaviour all their lives due to their affluence, background and upbringing. It is quite possible that such persons may experience a high degree of mental torture and strain if they have to face outrageous rudeness and lack of form in dealings with people. If that be so in their case, unmannerly behaviour in front of them would tantamount to some form of cultivated torture and may very well be included within the purview of a serious social lapse.

Apart from the fact that lack of etiquette is apt to spoil the show in any set-up, it may breed secret animosity and ill-feeling.

A person who behaves badly with another may not have the sense to take in the full implication of the insult offered by him to the other person. The aggrieved person, however, seldom forgets the source of his humiliation on a particular occasion and in his own way and capacity may try forever to retaliate and stand in the way of the person who had rubbed him the wrong way. The most serious effect of lack of etiquette is on the personality of the person who has this deficiency. He may be handsome, well-dressed and presentable in all respects but one single act of improper behaviour that may cause eyebrows to be raised may shatter the very impression that he was trying to make. Of all polished manners, nothing is so impressive as when a person is able to act in a natural way all through. The secret of becoming natural is the acme of etiquette which is a matter of practice and experience.

Why is lack of etiquette to be denounced? The answer is that it is double-edged. It harms the person who is without etiquette and also it puts others to avoidable embarrassment since they have to withstand the fortuitous action without any remedial course open to them. The remedy in such a case is to deal with the rude or impolite person strongly and turn him out of the company or shun his company forthwith. Since such a course of action is not always open to the company that is forced to endure unseemly behaviour, there may be displeasure and a feeling of harassment settling like a fog on all those present.

It cannot be denied that it may be difficult for a person to be master of all types of situations and there are likely to be some

CORRECT MANNERS AND ETIQUETTE

CORRECT MANNERS AND ETIQUETTE

occasions, however few they may be, where he may be desperately seeking help with regard to proper protocol. Even in such extraordinary situations which may arise once in a while in a man's life, he may sail through easily if he keeps his head and his wits about him. If he is confronted with a situation like meeting a very high dignitary all of a sudden, having to speak extempore before a gathering, escorting somebody or taking part in a ceremony, and so on, where he feels that he does not possess the required know-how, he has to acquire the habit of admitting his deficiency without losing face. If he can maintain general good behaviour and good grace all along the line, while doing his best to compensate for the lack and make things right, there is hardly any chance that he will cause dissatisfaction in any quarter.

Disadvantages

Learning is a great virtue and a large part of this learning consists in the will to learn. A person can go on adding to his knowledge of etiquette only when he has the simplicity of mind to face all situations and learn the best from them. The main disadvantages of lack of etiquette crop up because some people refuse to learn and keep their bad manners rather than do something to rectify the same. Due to their sloth and indifference, such people are apt to be left behind in the stream of cultural advancement that may do them material good.

The art of forging ahead in life is a great secret and a large part of the effort called for must come from the cultivation of good behaviour. Much of a person's deficiency is forgotten or forgiven if he has the right art of finesse to carry his message to others. There are talented persons who fret and fume and are left behind, while others with smaller endowments make the grade only because the latter are not stiff-collared or pig-headed and deal sincerely and respectfully with others. Where arguments and appeals fail, a smile may win the day. Once a person takes to grumbling, there is no end to it. What one should guard against is the temptation to ventilate one's resentment. It is not resentment that should be emphasised but the best way is to get over it.

Good manners and impatience rarely go hand in hand. Sobriety and invincibility are the two main ancillaries of good behaviour. The cares and anxieties of the ups and downs of life come fairly evenly to all. Only the ill-mannered person may go berserk at every step and create a calamity at every turn and shatter his life, while a man with good manners may be able to cut these short at their very inception. A man's popularity comes from his manners. In business or in service, in politics or in daily life, it is consideration for others that raises a man head and shoulders above his fellowmen. This secret of success is lost to those who would like to tarry and bicker and have their selfish ends achieved rather than yield an inch to the other fellow. This kind of total involvement with one's self is the main hurdle that impedes a man's development in any sphere. Aloofness is one thing, though it may not be recommended, but selfishness may well be termed a sin. A man without etiquette imposes himself on others and this form of social domination is the very offence that a cultivated man would strive to avoid.

Deficiency of Personality

If we compare the calm, impeccable man with one who is fidgety, irritable and easily excited, we shall know which of the two has a better personality. The formation of right personality goes a long way in helping a man to lead a normal and unperturbed life. The vagaries of life cannot be eliminated, but there is no sense in aggravating them. Misfortunes come and go but their impact may be softened to a great extent if a person has the right personality to tackle them. What is more, some or nearly all misfortunes may be turned to one's advantage if one can correctly respond and know how to profit by one's mistakes.

A personality cannot develop properly where there is no support from a strong character. Invariably, the question of character crops up because without a good character, good manners and correct etiquette would be superfluous. Without a good moral or ethical base, good manners may be transient and a person's politeness may degenerate into ruthless incivility at his first encounter with opposition. When politeness changes into rudeness at a moment's notice, a man's personality breaks up like a mask of clay and all his real ugliness is revealed. Handsome is that handsome does is not only a pithy saying but it is also a preamble for any man of good manners.

A man's background may be of great help or it may be a hindrance to the building up of his personality through the husbanding of etiquette. While a congenial background, nobility or bearing may be a good prop to this virtue, the incumbent's own efforts in this direction cannot be minimised. It is when a man rises above the muck and mire of his surroundings through his will and mental determination that he is able to give himself a permanent personality which may remain impenetrable to every thrust. Etiquette, therefore, is not merely theoretical training, it has to be tested and perfected in all our physical and worldly contacts. In this, as in every other thing, we have to allow ourselves to be caught young. Our family, our institutions, our friends, relatives and superiors lend their helping hand in giving us the much-needed poise in society, but above everything else, it is our own endeavour that is important in the long run.

CHAPTER ONE

General

*T*he bearing, the disposition, the demeanour and the poise determine the pattern of our life from our childhood. A man may stand erect or stoop, he may sit smartly or he may sit slouched and in a slovenly manner, he may speak nicely and soothingly or he may speak indistinctly or crudely. There is etiquette for parties and ceremonies and games. The rival captains, tennis stars and boxers shake hands and embrace each other and are not expected to lose temper in any contingency. A person is said to be in command of diverse situations if and when he is conversant with all the varieties of etiquette called for in our lives.

Etiquette in all Circumstances

When we speak of etiquette in general, we may not distinguish it from the overall good manners. As a child, one should learn to keep one's bearing and dignity in all circumstances. There are bedroom manners and drawing-room manners, manners at home, school and outside but there are also manners in everything else. It is said that a person is known by the way he quarrels because in quarrels his breeding comes out best. The essence of etiquette lies in self-control, the exercise of which has to be initiated early in life. It is difficult for any person to maintain his etiquette even in a homogeneous environment, if he lacks training in self-control.

Self-control in this sense should be permanent and not casual or artificial. The cheat or the swindler has the best of manners but only for a transient period. He is a fraud and he acts to impress only the simple-minded and the gullible. Real manners would make a man behave naturally and his very normalcy in a host of different circumstances shows his inherent culture. He never imitates. He may have learnt a variety of manners but in the cohesion of all types of different manners and right actions lies his art which he perfects in conformity with his own nature and upbringing. The cultivated man is aware of all the paraphernalia of etiquette under different situations. He knows the etiquette of welcoming and entertaining people as also the etiquette of bidding them farewell. He speaks with his friends in one tone and with his relatives in another and yet another while talking to his superiors and still a different and benevolent one while dealing with his juniors or inferiors, but the overall effect that he produces is that of cordiality which helps others to behave naturally and with confidence with him. The tacit encouragement afforded to others is implicit in his behaviour which prompts the former to open up before him. Such a man in giving of his best to others draws out also the best that is in the latter.

Notwithstanding the fact that the mastering and accumulation of etiquette for different human relations in society are the main goal for anyone out to shine in this direction, it is the comprehensive and integrated personality catering to the demands of all forms of man-to-man dealings that is most appreciated. If a man is a good socialiser, he has also to learn the art of living by himself, and his method of finding peace within himself, of having his tendencies and inclinations in hand and under discipline, is what lends him his maximum social credibility and acceptance.

Sitting

For a person appearing for an interview for a job, one of the first things he must learn is to sit properly. His hands are particularly important because when a person is in a sitting position, it is his hands, more often than not, that pose a problem for him if he is not well-versed in knowing how to deal with them. The way he puts out his hands may mark the quality of his character and his nature. If he is of a nervous disposition, he may very well find his hands getting in the way of presenting a calm front. Sometimes his nervousness or his tension may be apparent from the tremor, slight or noticeable, through his hands. He has, therefore, to learn how to place his hands properly either on the handles of the chair, on his lap or on the table in front of him.

Next in importance are the legs which have also to fall in place to give the man the required composure and self-assurance. Shaking one's legs while seated or making other movements may cause vibrations to his whole body which may be jarring on the interviewers. 'Sitting pretty' is thus not only a phrase that is to be by-passed but practised with spirit to bring about the best result. Also, it is to be borne in mind that the art of sitting is not an end in itself because a person may have to continue his conversation in this position, and while he may have presented a good picture while sitting, he should be careful that this picture is not adversely affected when he starts talking. He must talk without in any way disrupting his sitting position and see to it that he can talk pleasantly and concentrate on his talk without having others' attention distracted by his sitting position.

If a person is self-conscious, it is likely that he may not express himself without disturbing his sitting posture. Slight movements of the body including hands and feet may not be noticeable as long as he talks, if such movements are well synchronised and project his personality to advantage. These movements are to aid and promote his conversation and may be quite appropriate to his smoking, his laughter and his show of wonderment. But just as the dancer stops with the stopping of music, the person concerned should also be at repose as soon as his own words end. He must also manage his smiles, acknowledgements, nods and so on even with his sitting position which has to be combined with all these reactions.

Thus the interviewee may display his self-confidence or lack of it from the position he adopts while sitting. Those in command may have their heads in the air, their chests puffed out and their legs crossed at outstandingly protruding angles. The opposite of this may be observed from the bowed head and shoulders, hands between knees, and feet flat on the floor. Between these two extremes, there is a normal manner of sitting which does not give conspicuous airs this way or that. It is better to try to adopt the manner of keeping oneself in one's seat and be free from any showing-off or any cowering.

Standing

Standing is sometimes more difficult than sitting. One reason for this is that standing, whether prolonged or otherwise, causes more strain and a person is more vulnerable when standing than when sitting. The various lines of his body including the cut of his clothes are in sharp focus to the viewers and a standing man may not be in a convenient position all the time to vindicate his claim to good manners. However, a standing man may find it more easy to keep himself in control and confidence than when he is seated. This is more so when a person is used to standing— like guards, teachers, public speakers and so on. At the same time, there are others like receptionists, waiters, etc., who may have to practise the art of standing, since this pertains to their profession. The interviewee, on the other hand, has to know how to stand properly for being scrutinised before being asked to have his seat.

There are various modes of standing that a person may adopt—such as standing straight with his hands on both sides or with feet a little apart with his hands locked behind; or a little stooping or bowing as a mark of respect and so on. There is also the practice of some people who would like to stand with their fists on their waist and it is needless to point out that this is the worst form of standing and proves that the incumbent has no manners at all. To stand with one's hands on one's waist shows apparent disrespect to others and an indifferent attitude and should be avoided on formal occasions. One should try to practise a natural way of standing, with the hands hanging loosely at the sides. However, when a person is dealing with or looking after or taking care of a V.I.P., it would be better if he can adopt a posture of readiness instead of one of absolute composure and complacence.

While a person is in conversation with another person while standing, it is necessary that both should pay full attention to each other and should not have their attention diverted by other things. When two persons are wrapt in conversation, they present a pretty picture and look impressive to others. Certainly, if one of these two persons is the host at a ceremony and has the responsibility of welcoming or seeing to the convenience of many people at the same time, it may be permissible for him to look hither and thither or divide his attention while in conversation. Normally, it will be better for a person to be attentive to the talk in progress while he is conversing in a standing position. This he should do sincerely without giving an impression of self-consciousness or arrogance.

Speaking

Since most of our social contacts may be said to have been attained through the process of speech, it is more than relevant that a person, in order to have training in etiquette, should know first of all how to speak in a correct manner. The most important part of speech, whether private or public, is the form of address.

If the first address is soothing and impressive, much of the purpose may have been served. Generally, if a person has the right approach or method of address, it is almost certain that he will gain his objective.

Speaking is the main ingredient of good manners and the art of speaking softly and gently to produce a feeling of maximum civility is to be acquired like any other art. The way a person speaks can go a long way in bringing him success in life. There are people who may speak as if they own the world and their very approach to people on any subject is sure to provoke resentment in the latter. The former, however, may not be blamed since it may be that they never had the requisite training in this field, and so for them it is the brash or boastful approach that may appear to be most effective.

No one has to be a psychologist to know that every other person craves respect and as long as his self-respect is boosted up, he will do almost anything with grace and ease. Certainly there is the relationship of payer and payee, but even then if the former assumes that since he is the paymaster he has the right to command at will and hurt another's self-respect, he will be committing the greatest blunder. The utmost amount of work can be got out of an employee or somebody under obligation through cajoling and good behaviour and most of all through sweet words.

There is, however, a difference between genuine and artificial sweetness of tongue. There may be people who are endowed with a great power of speech and they may foolishly use their gift of the gab to cast a spell on others. Such a spell is short-lived in the long run and the smooth-tongued person is exposed and may lose face forever. The first step in good manners, nevertheless, should be concerned with the manner of speech that has to be adopted in different situations. Whether with friends, kinsmen or others, a person's voice and manner of speech should be soothing. It should be appealing without being servile, firm without being offending and polite without being demanding.

If proper attention is paid to one's speech, one will realise that one should never speak from the lips but from the heart and head. A person may be said to be speaking from lips when he is babbling out whatever comes readily to his mind. A more conscientious man would weigh his words and speak only what is reasonable and relevant. Some people, again, may entertain the notion that one should not suppress truth and, however painful it may be, it has to be spoken out. There is no denying that they are right, but at the same time, it is equally true that avoiding what is painful would do away with much misery of which there is already plenty in the world. Thus, the rule we should follow in our speech, in our private as well as public dealings is that hurting others is to be avoided at all costs, because, as the saying goes, the wound made by words goes deeper.

Games

The footballer who kicks another unnoticed, the chess player who takes advantage of the opponent's distraction, the participant in the party games who cheats only for the fun of it, and the youngster who bats but does not bowl, are all breaking the code of ethics which true sportsmen always uphold. Our lives in the ultimate analysis turn out to be some kind of a game and a person who is accustomed to cheat on the playing field may find it difficult to adjust himself in the great game of life. On the other hand, a person who has fought and scored either for his team or for himself most certainly retains that habit of fighting back squarely and fairly in all contingencies. Sports and games are essential parts of our life and education and these have to be integrated with our own life and not viewed as something separate from it.

The child who had been afraid to face his rival fairly and according to rules on the field may hardly find it convenient in life to face the struggle for existence later. It is wrong to think that affluence will dispel obstacles and difficulties from o ir lives. A man who is afraid may always be so unless he is dete mined to cure himself of this malady, and unless he does so, little inconveniences and petty grievances may upset him and make him seek the help of others. A child has thus to be taught to fight his battles himself, and nowhere can he learn this lesson better than on the playing field or in whatever games he may be interested to play.

So games have their ethics, their own code of conduct. A certain story goes that in a vital and decisive football match, the referee secretly favouring one side blew the whistle for a penalty against the other side. The sheer injustice of the decision was apparent from the huge volley of protests from the spectators' gallery. The captain of the team winning the penalty took the shot. Instead of shooting at the rival goal, he took a long kick and sent the ball flying into mid-field. The applause that rose was tremendous. Whether that team won or lost was immaterial. What was significant was that this captain established the highest ethical code for a sportsman on the field.

Training in games means taking victories and defeats in one's stride; as an English poet has said, 'Play, play, play the game'. We shall make inadequate sportsmen of ourselves if we aim only at victories, and victories by fair means or foul. It is only when we acquire the moral stamina of accepting our defeats and congratulating the winners without rancour or idea of revenge in our minds that we may be said to have acquired the true spirit of sportsmanship.

Parties

Those who have the good fortune to attend innumerable social functions and parties, without spite and without end may get fed up in the end or become so habituated to them that a new party may not bring any sensation of pleasure or thrill to them. Party etiquette is, therefore, equally applicable to these habitual party-goers as well as to others who may get a chance to attend parties once in a blue moon, because the experienced may become so accustomed that they may pay very little attention to their manners which may require to be polished from time to time, just as the inexperienced ones may totally lack party manners through which they may be accepted into the party circles.

The first thing to be remembered for those who take to parties as fish takes to water, is that they should not allow themselves to get stale because the moment they become uninteresting or long-faced, they forfeit their claim to attend the party. The gloom that they bring upon the gaiety around them may dampen others' spirits and the party may flop with no merriment for anyone and the cost and efforts of the host will all be wasted. If one is feeling low and not upto the mark for merriment expected at a party, such a person should keep away on some pretext, and no matter how flimsy his excuse may be for not joining the party, this situation is more welcomed than the attendance of a dispirited and unwilling participant.

In a party, one has to learn to let oneself go. Socialising, sharing, joy and exhilaration are the best aims of any party. People coming to a party should, therefore, contribute their best to make the party a success. This contribution should not be forced but should be a voluntary process which may enable a person to let the lighter side of life ooze out of himself to provide whatever diversion he or she is capable of giving to others. Music rises to its crescendo, to its highest pitch step by step and gradually. If there is a sudden rise of tempo in the music, it may be jarring on the nerves, and may fail to produce the desired effect. Similarly, party mixing should proceed gradually, acquiring more and more intensity and sense of intimacy as the party advances. However, once the party is on, there should be no more looking back, no more reservations or holding back, and participants are expected to open up and blossom to their maximum.

The main etiquette concerning a party is the attitude of the participants after the party is over. While the party lasts, a person may shout, jump, dance or make jokes, or in parties where strong drinks are served, he may become tipsy and talk a little loosely. All these are to be taken in the party spirit, realising that this very participant has been lending his share to save the party and there should be gratefulness to him from all, instead of raised eyebrows or criticism. There are, however, limits to the game and a person attending a party should know the limit and where he should draw the line. Nothing more is needed to ruin a party than that one of the participants should become sick or lose control over himself. Anyway, it would be regarded as among the worst of manners to refer to the revelries and misbehavior, if any, of any participant afterwards, especially in sober moments the next day or thereafter. A party is a party and we should be able to keep our daily life and manners separate from our sayings and doings in a party.

Social Discourse

It is said that a man may do without his friends and relatives but he cannot do without his neighbours. As a member of society, every person has his duties to discharge not only to himself but also to others with whom he comes in contact in the course of his work or life. In furtherance of that argument, it may also be pointed out that though a man may live singly or separately, those living near or about him have a right to know something about him, his habits, his work and so on. If a neighbour's eye is probing through my open window, I may withstand it with a neighbourly spirit because I have to prove my acceptance in society by the fact that I am living according to the social norms and am not a criminal or a pervert.

Certainly, a man has his right to privacy and no peeping Tom is tolerated in any locality, but this idea of privacy differs from place to place and from country to country, nay from one stratum to another within the same community. Generally, too much privacy may be looked upon with suspicion, and though there is much reticence in cities than in villages regarding how things are with the Joneses, the people living next door may have the right to know, within reasonable limits, a few things about their neighbours. The social etiquette that would endear one to one's neighbour, generally speaking, would mean the knowledge how far one should allow one's neighbour ordinarily to come close to oneself. If one is following the right path of relationship with one's neighbours, one has every right to put one's foot down when some of the neighbours seek to become too intimate unreasonably.

At the same time, we have all to realise that our standing in society is fulfilled to its maximum only when we live in cooperation and co-existence with others. It is common etiquette to render whatever assistance is possible to one's fellowmen. Such behaviour has a double advantage, first, the neighbours and others in their turn are somewhat obligated to help the former person if he happens to be in a difficulty, and second, a person acquires a moral character to face the world and establish himself in society. Whether help is forthcoming or not from those quarters to whom assistance had been rendered previously is not of importance, but what is essential for one's proper bringing up and self-improvement is to stand by others in their distress or hour of need.

Ceremonies

Cultural and religious ceremonies are special occasions and everybody concerned should bring forth his best to give the required tone and spirit to the ceremony. In a religious ceremony which is supposed to be an important day in the life of the community, it will be wrong to throw cold water on others, particularly young folks. Sometimes we may feel that some of the trimmings of a certain ceremony may be done away with, but it may be held that cultural and religious ways cannot be judged in parts but in their entirety. If we have to take part in a ceremony of this nature, we have to follow the whole process in letter and in spirit because the feeling of belonging and of mutual love generated through minor ways may be more important for the members of the community for being brought together in some deep, intimate way.

Such type of ceremonies come once in a while or even if they are frequent, it is very easy to rouse common understanding and fraternity through these ceremonies since the ways and means are generally known to all. The main endeavour should be to go with the crowd and mix with it. Where this will is present, it is not difficult for a layman to have his due share of fun and frolic. Good nature and easy disposition are the ingredients of the ceremonial personality, and with a little self-control, hitches and altercations may be avoided easily, making it the duty of all to see that untoward incidents are kept at bay during the ceremony. In ceremonies, where gaiety is the keynote by virtue of its being an auspicious occasion, all personal sorrows and grievances are to be shelved and in their place encouragement, congratulations, blessings and happiness should pour forth from all directions. The habit of mixing comes in very handy in these instances because while everybody contributes to make the ceremony joyous, a few repartees and mild repercussions may have to be withstood sometimes for the sake of social contact. A profusion of smiles and the power to return jokes would enable a person to be readily accepted in a circle in which he may find himself. However, easy though it may appear, the adoption of this type of simple and open attitude would require much practice and participation in similar ceremonies.

Professions

Every profession has its own etiquette towards customers and the general public. The lawyer has to maintain his professional ethics by keeping the secrets of his clients. The doctor has to keep to himself the ailments of his patients. There are other professions which call for secrecy. Where these secrets are not maintained, legal steps may be taken against the offender and the latter may be penalised. Apart from customers and clients, the aforementioned professionals have their duties to the public no less than to their countrymen. If a theft is detected or the guilty person is apprehended, the lawyer in the locality may have to take the initiative. Similarly, if a person is sick in a crowd, the doctor in the gathering has to come forward. If there is engine trouble on the way and passengers are stranded, the engineer or the technician has to rush voluntarily to help.

Professionals are generally in an advantageous position. This theory may not be true where the competition is more intense, but in a place where a single professional is the sole consultant, it is not difficult for him to fleece people and make unjustified profits. Unless such a professional is endowed or imbued with a sense of duty, service and national spirit, he may hold the common people to ransom. The temptations to turn crooked may be many; the trials and tribulations to lead a person astray may be numerous but the professional can prove his true worth and vindicate himself by keeping to his principles without which he may be regarded as a social evil rather than a social necessity.

The compassion and consideration that a professional shows to those who turn to him for help and guidance increase the goodwill and faith of his clientele in him. It is when a professional plays false that his customer may turn elsewhere for redress and this will not only affect the latter materially but may cause him to have his hopes in mankind shattered forever, leading to a process of moral degeneration. The professional's responsibility to his community is infinite and since he is looked upon as a leading member of society, he should give his reputation and self-respect priority over all other considerations.

Service

When a young man secures a job which is to his liking he does not realise that this is the beginning of a long line of rights and duties which he has to follow and implement. The etiquette of getting along with people is of primary importance in any service. A person who is efficient at his job and also mixes freely with his colleagues and others is sure to evoke in his employer some interest in him. Such an employee may get even difficult things done more easily than another who is more efficient but is of an aloof and indifferent disposition. In the house or at the office the maximum efficiency would depend upon coordination with and cooperation from others. A person would commit the greatest blunder to think that he and he alone can perform all the tasks and show himself to be a paragon of efficiency. No matter how outstanding he may be, his principle of working single-handedly cannot be accepted and thus the successful executive is one who has the art of getting the best work out of those working under him. This goes for an ordinary employee as well, who has to be at peace with others in the office to do his own duties as well as persuade others to do things for him. An employee, whether a superior or a subordinate, may find nobody prodding him on if he knows his place and does not step out of it. Also, mixing does not entitle an employee to indulge in unnecessary gossip and waste of his own time as well as that of others. An office is not a recreation centre and so whatever palatable talk or informative discussion is going on, the same is seldom appreciated by those who are mere listeners. The objective in the office is 'work' and

29

each employee has a duty to see that maximum work is done under his charge with high efficiency. If work is taken as the main function of an office, other things including small and petty quarrels may pale into insignificance.

Service before self is the underlying etiquette that runs through the whole gamut of the working world. Each person in this set-up has to be aware of his position, status and responsibilities in relation to others in their respective fields. Respect for others and mutual appreciation are the dual tenets of the behaviour-line in service. It would be wrong to put on airs because one has been entrusted with more work. Everybody in the office and the service line has his or her individual share of the 'clog in the wheel'. The machinery cannot move even if a single and minute item or part is missing. Everybody counts, and in this big field of action, one has to be suppliant to the superior, just as one has to be understanding and patient with those who are subordinates.

CHAPTER TWO

Family

*C*harity begins at home is an adage which indicates that one has to learn to show consideration to members of one's family before extending humanity to outsiders. The family is the basic closely-knit unit in any community. It grows under the fostering cocoon-like spinning and contribution of different members in the family. If the relationship between the different members *inter se* is built on the sound foundations of love and mutual assistance, children and adults alike may grow to fulfil themselves in life. The father, the mother, the brothers, the sister, the servants, and even the pets have their own place in the family and the proper etiquette that may be stressed in the family is to behave in a manner, that is, speak and act, so as not to hurt another member but to encourage him or her for betterment.

Father

It is needless to say that as head of the family, the father has the maximum responsibility in the family. Chanakya, the renowned Indian statesman and economist of ancient times, held that as the head of the family is, so will the different members of the family be. The father may not be aware of it but each member in the family under him is watching the next step that he is taking or is about to take. Certainly, this phenomenon has greatest intensity when the father's wards have not come of age, but if the father has trained them well, his sons and daughters may regard him forever as a great and grand preceptor or counsellor in all contingencies.

The father has to set the rules of etiquette in the house and has himself to follow them truly and fully. He has to teach the children to greet one another pleasantly and be respectful towards their parents. At the same time he cannot successfully implement this with the help of the whip but he has to establish it by setting an example—by greeting everybody, even the youngest member and behave with the latter with proper dignity. Children are tiny, sensitive souls. They are like soft clay which may be moulded whichever way one wishes. If the father behaves roughly with them at each new encounter, the child's ego may get hurt and it is possible that the child may develop a variety of complexes when it grows up. In line with this principle, it would be wrong to order one's children about and treat them in the same way as servants or subordinates.

A laughing, friendly and encouraging father may achieve a lot in his children than another adept in all other arts but lacking in these essential qualities. It would be preposterous for a father to talk of honesty and preach the same if he himself practises dishonesty and corruption. The same is the case with courage and cowardice. The father has to stand at the helm of affairs in all situations. He has to steer the family clear of troubled waters by his own grit. Certainly other members of the family are expected to lend whatever assistance they can to the head but it would be the latter's responsibility to carry on, on his own, just as it would be the duty of the other members to come forward and silently stand by their chief.

An example of the father's role at the breakfast table:

Child: Good morning, Father (Dad or Pop), good morning, Mother (Mom or Ma).

Father: Good morning, son. Did you have good sleep?

Child: Yes, thank you. Please pass me the salt, Dad. (Then biting into some food and speaking to Mother) May I have some more jam, Mom?

Father: Ah-ha, talking again with your mouth full, mind that, son.

Child: I'm sorry, Dad.

Mother

Give me good mothers and I will give you a good nation, Napoleon was said to have remarked once. Without the mother's benevolent touch and artistry, no family can grow properly, much less advance in this strife-ridden world. The sweetness and warmth of the mother permeates into the hearts of all the members of the family. The father may be the formal head of the family but it is the mother who brings up the family and trains the young. Just as the baby and the toddler learn to articulate in the mother's language, so also do they learn from the mother the essential etiquette in life. There is no crime more heinous than to forget this contribution of the mother in one's life. It is the mother who teaches the child how to behave generally and with others. If by any chance the mother, due to ignorance or otherwise, transmits her wrath or feeling or revenge to the child, it may grow up to be a miserable person afterwards. The child has no manners, it will learn whatever it is taught, and it is only the mother's watchful eye that can detect where and when the child is going wrong.

She looks after the small details of personal cleanliness, preservation of mental and physical health, ways of sitting, standing and speaking in a comely and becoming manner. Her rebukes and chidings are handy and all mothers must be firm with a misbehaving child, but motherly love and encouragement count most. The mischief done in the tender years of childhood may not be taken too seriously unless bad habits start forming in the child in a deep-rooted way. Nor is the policy of taking everything to daddy to be applauded. A mother who complains frequently or is too strict may herself be instrumental in losing her hold on her children. She who relies on her motherly instincts does not lack the knowledge as to when to give in and when to hold out in dealing with her children. The home should be a place for cooperation, not conflict, and harmony between mother and father is necessary for the implementation of any rule or principle and in this connection in the face of any strong strictures from the father, it is for the mother to distinguish encouragement from indulgence.

The mother, putting her child to bed:

Mother: Good night, Darling. Sweet dreams.

Child: Good night, Mom.

Mother: Don't forget your prayers.

Child: No Mom, I won't. Mom, I love you so.
Mother: Sleep well, darling.

Children

It is in the proper upbringing and development of children that the ideals of a family are fulfilled. Children must receive their first lessons in etiquette in the family and to propagate this the school and the home have to work in unison. It would be wrong for the parents to leave all the responsibility to the educational institution in the upbringing of their child. Even if the child is put in the best of institutions, the parents or guardians are to keep a watch and see that the child does not take a turn in life for the worse.

In the home itself, the child learns how to behave with the different age-groups and the various relatives and acquaintances. A child should be taught to address elders in a respectful manner. A precocious and demonstrative child may be interesting to watch but when the limits of civility and orderliness are exceeded, a child may become a disturbing element to an outsider and embarrassing to its parents. The fault, however, may not lie with the child itself but with those who are supposed to be in charge of it. A misbehaving child should at once be taken to task, whether in a public or in a private place. A wrong once overlooked tends to multiply, but when it is checked as its first occurrence, it may disappear forever.

The child may possess all its instincts and inclinations in the raw and hence it may commit or will be prone to commit one mistake after another. If the guardians lose hope easily and brand the child as mischievous or incorrigible, it is the child who would be lost, indeed. It is well to remember that a child is liable to correction even upto the adolescence age. Anyway, the hope for the correction of a child should never be given up. Even in the face of gross and continued misbehaviour if the parents persevere to bring the child round for its correct development, much good may be done. It is, at least, better than giving up and not lifting one's finger in this direction.

Gentle words, politeness, discipline, obedience, sense of duty, personal cleanliness, manners in eating, standing and so on and so forth which a child is taught in its early and impressionable years are the responsibilities of parents and guardians. The child must not touch other's things; it should not interfere and pass opinions when elders are conversing; it should keep its mouth shut while chewing food; it should not acquire dirty habits like sucking fingers or putting them in nostrils, etc; it should not fidget, nor should it be rude; it should not be present in the company of elders longer than necessary; it should know its position in the family and in any company. It should also be taught to say its prayers regularly, to say good night, good morning, etc., to wait its turn at table and not grab food out of turn, to show respect to the opposite sex, to have compassion for one who is weaker. A child which turns into a bully is a coward at heart and is a loser in any competition.

These details of daily dealings and the manners of regular living are not to be made mechanical and hence strictness should also have its limits, and admonitions and rebukes are to be aptly punctuated by love, faith and mutual trust. The rigours of discipline and etiquette are not to be viewed individually but in their entirety, in conformity with the personality of the child concerned. Repeated stress on something may not be required in the case of a child who is sensitive and is basically of a responsible nature. Development in a child is thus at once the simplest and also the hardest, depending on the attitudes and allowances that a parent or guardian is capable of making in relation to a child.

Attendants

Many families would not be complete without a whole retinue of servants, attendants, helpers and so on. The ideology of democracy has prompted the origination of small families and hence these other persons may be found to be superfluous in a modern family. All the same, the different manners and relationship between these various types of other persons who may be attached to a family require another code of conduct which is to be followed for the purpose of civil behaviour. The differences between the different kinds of attendants and between the attendants and menials have to be clearly delineated. Sometimes an attendant, especially if he or she is of the companion type, is well-educated and competent in all respects and should command a different behaviour from all, including other members in the employer's family.

To such a person, servants and subordinates should never show disrespect and should know how to keep their places regarding the former. At the same time the former should also not behave in a high and mighty manner and should be able to maintain a poise of detached friendliness with the subordinates in the household. He should on, no account, pose himself to be in the same category as that of the head and other members of the family. It would not behove him to boss over the servants because he does not have a strong claim to their service. It would be advisable for him or her to inspire cooperation and trust in those under him in the household or those who are to look after him. It is not for him to command but to request, not to be angry but to be patient, not to be irritable but to be charming, not to be sombre but to be good-humoured.

In a big and aristocratic household in spite of the different gradations of the persons attached to the family, those in the rank of attendants and helpers or companions do not always have rigid rules of behaviour, except that they have to be pleasant, sincere, devoted and easy to get along with. Certainly he or she cannot participate in close family discussions and get involved in intimate family affairs. Yet the extent of closeness that such a person may attain will depend on this person's own personality. If by his personality, behaviour and culture, this person proves himself to be superior to the general lot of his class, he may be brought very close to the family's life and may be asked to deliver his opinion on important occasions.

The children and young people in the family have to be taught to have proper regard for such a person in the family whom they have to treat rather as a guest and a well-wisher than anything else. In fact, children of the family can learn many good things of life from such a person, who has already established himself in the family as an epitome of virtue. It may also be held for this person that since there is no hard and fast rule of behaviour for their kind, a person of this status may behave with as much dignity as he or she is capable of, provided that behaviour stays within the purview of civility and does not descend to haughtiness or insolence.

Servants

It may be wrong for a servant to brood over his assignment or employment in the family and consider himself a dejected and cast-off person. A servant has a very important part to fulfil in family life. If the parents are professionals or are both office-goers or otherwise preoccupied, it is the servant or servants whom the children may look up to during their growing stage. Sometimes the affinity between the elderly servant, male or female, and the young ones in the family becomes so deep and irrevocable that it may reach even a far nobler realm than the ordinary parent-child relationship.

However, not all the servants may boast of or hope to attain such an exalted position in the family, as it would require outstanding qualities in the servant, like love, sacrifice, perfection and even saintliness, because at the aforementioned level of attainment, the servant may place service before self in the most literal sense and achieve some amount of super-human disposition. For the servant, nevertheless, there are somewhat fixed rules of conduct. The first is that a servant should never forget his position. No matter how he performs or in what friendly manner he is treated, he should never forget that the master is the boss and the two positions cannot be at par. If he is able to maintain his distance (not materially because he may be sitting on the same couch with the master and taking the same food, but theoretically and invisibly), he initiates the feeling of trust in the master.

The second important thing for the servant to be acquainted with is to know when to appear and when to disappear from the scene. This calls for experience and a sense of loyal service. A servant should acquire the art of silently slipping away when he has nothing conspicuous to do and appearing the moment his absence is felt. Also, the master wants work and not adulation and though the latter may be at times necessary and pleasing to the master, only a foolish master will retain a very inefficient servant unless this is due to compassion and charity. The most important of all things for a servant to remember is that he should keep no secrets from his master within the periphery of his service duties. He may at times use diplomacy or tact in dealing with others who are at variance with his master but he should never apply such tact against his own employer.

Here is an example of an ideal servant from George Bernard Shaw:

(Father of the house Petkoff discovers about daughter Raina's secret romance and determined to find out calls out to the servant, Nicola.)

Petkoff: ... Now you know there's something more in this than meets the eye; and I'm going to find it out. *Shouting*, Nicola!

Nicola: *Coming to him*, Sir!

41

Petkoff: Did you spoil any pastry of Miss Raina's this morning?

Nicola: You heard Miss Raina say that I did, Sir.

Petkoff: I know that, you idiot. Is it true?

Nicola: I am sure Miss Raina is incapable of saying anything that is not true, Sir.

Petkoff: Are you? Then I'm not...

(Here Bernard Shaw in *Arms and The Man* shows the level-headedness of the servant when he is caught in the cross-currents of contradictory whims of the members of the family.)

Guests

Every man is a host in his own house and a guest in another's unless he happens to be an intruder at the latter's. There are guests who continue to stay over being compelled to do so by circumstances and there are others who are invited to live with the family for a time during holidays, festival seasons and so on. As long as the guest is staying with the host's family, he or she has to abide by the rules of the household. There may be inclinations and intentions that they feel at the new place, which if roused at their own place, would have received full and free expression, but at the host's house, the guest has to suit his or her propensities to the discipline of the host's house. Certain individualistic traits cannot be avoided, however; otherwise the distinctness of a character will be obliterated forever. Thus, the guest may be more keen on reading than on enjoying outdoor life and activities. He may require a little more privacy for his relaxation. His food habits may be somewhat different from those of the family with whom he is staying. He may be allergic to certain kind of food. He may be shy or an extrovert. He may be carefree or he may be serious. In any event, in conformity with these proclivities, the guest has to adjust himself with everybody and everything in his new environment. There is one thing that he must try to achieve. He must forget his worries, throw his anxieties to the winds and turn out his most charming and cheerful self during the period of his stay.

Unless a family has trained itself well in the art of etiquette, there is apt to creep in a certain amount of complacency in the behaviour of the members of the family towards the guest, particularly when the stay is going to be long. It is needless to mention that all the members of the family including the head of the family should see to it themselves that drabness, monotony or indifference does not seep in gradually into their behaviour with the guest. At the same time, it is for the guest to keep in mind that he must leave the moment he has outlived his welcome. He must make some excuse and take himself off. He and his host's family have not clicked and the relationship has not blossomed into a mutual need. As an unwanted guest, the one and only thing that he can do is to say goodbye. However, it is common courtesy for the young and old in the family to show appropriate respect to the guest even though the family's ways and his own seem to clash and are different.

Neighbours

It is customary for all of us to have and maintain normal discourse with our neighbours. Unity is definitely a kind of strength for the families in a neighbourhood, because there may arise all sorts of difficulties and obstacles to the families jointly such as the growth of insanitation, the mischief of some miscreants, common nocturnal crimes like thefts and burglaries, etc.; in short, some common threat of any kind to all those living in the same locality. It is the neighbours who have to stand by one another at these times of distress and since no other person may realise this kind of threat or menace better than the neighbours themselves, it is for the neighbours to pool their resources together and stand united.

Greeting and smiling to one another, therefore, are to be the main duties among neighbours. Neighbours are likely to meet on the road, at the market or elsewhere, and an automatic greeting has to be given out and reciprocated. Raising one's hat or hand is the common practice abroad while passing by a neighbour, while in India, the same may be expressed in whatever way it is felt that courtesies can be exchanged. While greeting and smiling or some form of acknowledgement should not be avoided, it may be taken as bad manners for one neighbour to go beyond that ordinarily in respect of another. In line with this, it would be incorrect to ask a person where he is going while meeting him on the street, or to go into deeper and more intimate questions without being invited to do so. No hard and fast rule may be put down in this respect. The right behaviour would be different on different occasions, depending on the relationship between the two neighbours.

The general rule, however, is that unless volunteered, one neighbour should not go beyond the common civilities while speaking to another neighbour. The talk should proceed along open and general lines, like the weather, the economy of the country, sports and games, hobbies like gardening, and so on, and should seldom involve personal matters.

The different levels of society have different rules of neighbourliness. Those who are not affluent and lead a life of hardship and struggle may not care a straw for their secrets or their reputation, and it may be quite imaginable that in a locality composed of individuals of this similar trait, everybody may know the affairs of the other person, and the actions and reactions among all the persons in the neighbourhood may proceed as if everybody is a part and parcel of a big or gigantic family. This type of intimacy and closeness diminishes in proportion according to the standard of affluence and educational and cultural backgrounds of the members of the neighbourhood, ending at the higher-up stratum where one person may not be knowing or caring to know who is living next door.

The following are some of the do's and don'ts for neighbours:

1. Mr and Mrs X pay a visit to their new neighbours.

Mr X: Good evening. Sorry to bother you at this odd hour. We live next door to you on the right.

Mrs X and myself have been planning to come over for some time now. Hope we're not in the way.

Neighbour: Not in the least. Come in by all means. Good evening to you (shaking hands) and thank you for taking the trouble. We're having a second round of tea—mighty cold you know—would you care to join us?

2. Mrs M presses the front door-bell of the neighbour's house and the maid appears.

   Mrs M: I heard Mrs P (the mistress) is down with fever. How's she now?

   Maid: She's sleeping, ma'am, please come in.

   Mrs M: No, thank you, I would not like to disturb her. Please give her this note when she is feeling better.

   (In the note in an open envelope she had written: We are sorry to hear about your illness and are anxious for your quick recovery. We convey to you our serious concern. Sd/- Mr and Mrs M.)

3. Mrs A: Just saw Mrs So-and-So at the market. Couldn't recognise the young man she was going around with. Any cousin staying with her that you may know of?

   Mrs B: I know my limits and my rights, Mrs A, and if Mrs So-and-So is moving about with a young man or a young woman, she's jolly well within her rights; don't you think so?

   Mrs A: My word, you're flying off the handle right away. Well, I'll be seeing you—got to pick up my son from school...

CHAPTER THREE

Institution

I n building up the character and career of a child, the institution to which it is sent is most immediately involved. Though education is the main object of schools, yet the good principles imbedded in the imparting of education have to be appropriated by the student so that he may implement these in his practical life. Work, discipline, morality, regularity, openheartedness, physical development, cultural enhancement, cooperation, coexistence, sociability and a host of other important virtues are to be implanted in the minds of the young hopefuls. Institutions may not always achieve miracles but can expedite the process of mental growth that the child shows, or can fertilize the receptability that the child may already possess. How well these institutions can perform will depend on how well equipped they are with the necessary resources.

Head of institution

Like the head of the family, the head of the institution is and has to be the path-finder for his institution. He may or may not have direct contact with students all the time, but his interest and concern for the students and the well-being of all concerned may make all the difference. The rules and regulations of the school may be wide and extensive but without proper implementation, these rules may turn out to be quite useless, more so because among the students there may be no dearth of enthusiasm for breaking these rules! It is not only when rules are strict, but also when they are made to be obeyed strictly under the personal supervision of the head of the institution that these rules become really effective.

It is, therefore, imperative for the headmaster to make daily rounds to see that everything is in order and the rules formulated are followed in letter and spirit. To make this supervision more effective, it would be advisable for the headmaster not to keep to a steady schedule but to be out in the school corridors at all hours without notice and unexpectedly. This may keep everybody on his toes and the following of the regulations may proceed smoothly. Miscreants and mischief-mongers in the school should not go unpunished and their agonies and embarrassments should be made exemplary. But there should be equitable treatment for all, and though the more intelligent and brilliant ones may become favourites, those lagging behind in studies should not be neglected but encouraged, and there ought to be scope in a school to develop whatever good qualities a child may possess.

The headmaster is like a father to the institution and, therefore, he has within his fold not only students but teachers and others connected with the school. Nobody can or should question the authority and superiority of the headmaster, but he must have sympathy and respect for his teachers. It may be considered very bad manners to remonstrate or take to task a teacher in public or in the presence of students, because such action may demoralise the teachers and make the students indisciplined. The errant

49

teacher, if any, has to be called aside and spoken to and warned, if necessary, but before everybody his good qualities and his position have to be extolled. A good management does not call for altercations in the open before everyone but discipline should be generated through discussions and closed-door meetings.

Teachers

A teacher must try to be as perfect as he can. Indeed, we may realise how easy it is for students to follow their teacher and do everything he advises when they have complete faith in that teacher and know him to be someone above common frailties. The personal character and disposition of the teacher are good milestones for students, who, it is quite possible, would not only like to follow his teaching but also his example in almost all matters. Teaching is thus a great responsibility and it may amount to gross misconduct, indeed, if this vocation is taken lightly and carelessly. A teacher may not come upto the ideal standard since that would be almost an impossibility but he should be aware of the requirements and his own shortcomings in the matter.

A teacher is a human being, a person of flesh and blood but that has to be forgotten completely in the class-room. The teacher who has been able to keep apart the two sides of his personality, his normal self and his teaching self, may be at peace with himself, and may also give off his best to his students. It would be inappropriate for a teacher to take advantage of his superior position and turn or make use of his pupils to serve his own interests. The love and respect that he may wish to command from his students have to be spontaneous and should not be demanded under any sort of compulsion.

In the class-room and outside, a teacher is a teacher in relation to his students and he has by all means to keep to that status. A teacher who misbehaves and abuses students for nothing in the class-room or outside may not be considered fit for this position. It may be a mistake on the part of a teacher to fight with another teacher in the presence of students or to involve the latter in his personal affairs. There may be exceptional situations when students prompted by the love and regard they feel for their teacher may wish to know more about the teacher, his personal life and so on and at these times it would be reasonable for the teacher to open his heart to them, but the keynote is love and understanding of students and these must be the guiding factors in a teacher's career.

Students

It may sound preposterous and meaningless to lay down rules for students when they themselves are to be taught, coached and trained. Yet, there are students of all grades and ages, students belonging to colleges and universities, adult students belonging to institutions and organisations, and in fact among students we may include the whole class of individuals who may be receiving some sort of instruction from others. Barring infants, children and adolescents, the grown-up students should be in the know of the recognised codes of accepted behaviour *vis-a-vis* those from whom they acquire knowledge.

Students must realise that their teacher may not be perfect and unless they allow the teacher to be normal and concern themselves only with the volume and quality of the education they receive, they may not be able to establish the required relationship between themselves and their preceptor. Anybody who is treated with the teacher's dignity and commands trust and confidence from those who are being taught will naturally be able to give of his best to his students. This art of learning from the teacher is generally known to the intelligent and seriou student, but it is the average student who creates all the disturbances and may kick up a row about the teacher's alleged incompetence.

Students should remember that in the class-room the teacher is not a person but a teacher and so to indulge in rowdyism, disobedience or to show impertinence and so to harass the teacher is not at all expected of them. They must develop a sense of devotion, purpose and self-respect and no matter what diversions they may have normally to amuse themselves, these should have nothing to do with their place of study which they should always regard with the greatest awe and respect. They should regard their school as a temple of knowledge. In the same way, respect for teachers is a must for all students. In relation to their teachers, they have to remember the benefits they will receive from the latter.

Employees and Workers

The employees and the workers who are attached to institutions are also to distinguish themselves from their colleagues in other establishments. Institution workers have to cultivate a special kind of zeal and devotion for their work because along with teachers and instructors these workers, like school and college or office employees, have to deal with the young of the new generation in the country and their responsibility in helping young men and women cannot be belittled. It is common practice in many institutions and particularly with many students that they address members of the office staff of the institution respectfully as 'Sir'. If that be so, the employees have also to treat the members of the young generation of their institutions with due respect and guide or direct them properly.

These aforementioned persons should train themselves to acquire the necessary dignity so that starting from the chowkidar or the gate-keeper to the office superintendent, all should regard the institution as their very own and should work loyally to improve the level of the students in their organisation and take pride in such improvement. This mentality is more important in nurseries and primary schools than in places where students are older. But no matter what the ages of the students in the institution may be, everybody in the school should work for strictly maintaining the discipline of the institution. The wrongdoers should be appropriately reported for their misdoings and punished. A great responsibility rests on the gate-keeper of the institution who has been instructed not to let anyone out during school hours. The character or career of many students may be seriously harmed if any lapse occurs in carrying out such orders. Similarly, the office staff may be entrusted with the circulation of important circulars about examinations, tests, tutorials, sports, fees, tours and so on, all of which may have a great bearing on the lives of students. Institutional work requires a great sacrifice and social spirit without which and without the cooperation of the office staff in the institution, the progress of the students may be seriously retarded.

Parents

Children belong to society as a whole and in their proper development, the common action and intention of everybody in society are to be harnessed. Teachers and parents are directly involved in this process. The indifference and apathy of parents with regard to their children in the matter of education can be considered nothing less than a crime. When a parent gets his child admitted into a good institution and then shuts his eyes completely to his progress, there are chances that the child may or may not reach the desired standard of achievement. To make it a certainty, the parents have to be intimately involved in the performance and conduct of the child.

The parent-teacher relationship has to be based on a supplementary and complementary assignment. There is no scope for misunderstanding in this. There should be sympathy, mutual help and fellow-feeling. The teacher has to deal with a host of students, sometimes a very large number, and it is understandable that frail as human nature is, mistakes may happen in the teacher's action. It is for the parent to understand the work and burden of the teacher and help him in every way, so that his lack or shortcoming may become apparent to him and he may have the opportunity of retracing his steps or changing his method on the next occasion. On his part, the teacher has to keep in mind that the father or the guardian may have other responsibilities or he may have a big family, in which case it may not be possible for him to give individual care to every child in his charge.

In these aforementioned circumstances, if there is proper and timely cooperation between the teacher and the parent, they may meet at mutually convenient hours and solve things through discussions. To establish such a relationship, it is expedient for the parent as well as for the teacher not to lower each other in the student's eyes. The parent should build up at home the feeling that the teacher can do no wrong and really no matter what eccentricities a teacher may have, he is capable of contributing to the growth of students in a major way. Just as patience is required on the parent's part, the teacher has to use extreme tact in dealing with parents. In the ever-growing respect between these two stalwarts in a student's life, the latter's mental faculties blossom in full.

CHAPTER FOUR

Office

*T*he attitudes, actions and reactions of people working in an office have to be enumerated before we deal seriously or in any extensive way with official etiquette. There are large offices comprising floors, buildings and blocks, and there are also offices consisting of only one-room tenements. They may have luxurious and sophisticated furniture, or there may be only a table and a chair. The size and shape of offices may be different, but the form, manners and dealings in them are the same. Even if it is a one-room office, it is not the living abode of anyone, and, as such, things cannot be taken in a light-hearted manner. The visitor cannot look into or handle the documents lying on even a single table in the room, nor can he order the attendant about at random. Similarly, the subordinate cannot sit in the chair of the superior even if it be vacant or spend time in idle gossip on a rainy day when there is no work. In strict official routine, it may take hours, days or even months for one paper to move from one table to another adjacent to it. All these things and more are to be taken in and appreciated before an employee can become a successful office-worker.

Superiors

The relativity of the official status of the superior and the subordinate is amazing to anyone not initiated in the laws of the working world. There may be practically nobody who may be superior or inferior as such, because the same person may be superior to one and inferior to another, and so on the process goes backward and forward, upward and downward, and hence in the office almost everyone has to be conscious about the rights and duties that fall to his share both as a superior and as a subordinate. The main objective of an office is to produce something or supervise the production of something, and hence superiors have their exalted positions with much bigger responsibilities which they must discharge to the best benefit of their office or concern.

It is true that superiors in the office enjoy better facilities and amenities but their responsibilities are also greater and to retain their position successfully, they should not only be efficient and hardworking but should also possess the necessary tact, generosity, compassion and so on. Let us take the chief man in an office, the manager, for instance. The manager has multifarious responsibilities. He has to take work from those under him; he has to maintain proper goodwill and relationship with outsiders, customers and so on; he has to see to the administration and efficiency of the department or the organisation, as the case may be, besides shouldering innumerable other duties which are unclassified.

. The manager has to be genial, lenient, strict, vigorous, reserved, good-humoured, pliable and inflexible, as occasion demands, to those working under him. A manager cannot turn a deaf ear to the appeals and entreaties of other employees. He cannot curb the spirit of progress or block efficiency of his subordinates. He has to inspire cooperation, not command it. He has to provide scope and the right atmosphere for development of those who are loyal and deserving. He has to have personal knowledge of his staff and know how to get the best out of them. Civility is an asset to him, at the same time he cannot allow himself to be slack in his behaviour. He has to be gentle with the sensitive and overbearing with those who are rough and rugged. But he should not bear any grudge, should keep himself from getting involved in their affairs, personally or emotionally, either adversely or intimately.

Subordinates

Though superiors are there to order and manage, the work of the subordinates is no less important. The peon who cleans the master's table, the typist who types the letters for him and the driver who is attentive to his duties throughout the day and at times even at night are the most useful people in his working life. The work of the organisation may come to a standstill if all these people do not function in a well-knit or coordinated manner. Work is sacred and today's subordinate may have the possibility of becoming tomorrow's master. Despair and frustration are evils that eat into a subordinate's efficiency and have to be discouraged.

The important thing for the subordinate is to remember his place, the range of his duties and his limitations. Orders are to be carried out without question and the subordinate who fits himself into this operational preamble will automatically catch the eye of his master or at least will never go unnoticed. To know one's duties and to obey orders may not be so easy in the practical field, as it may appear in theory. There may be situations where the subordinate may have to use his own intelligence, or make decisions on his own. There is no doubt that these are small decisions but they are decisions all the same, and the subordinate who has taken the correct step once may go ahead in life doing the same.

There are curtsies that a subordinate has to extend to his superiors in the office. It is also customary for a subordinate to stand up and keep on standing when the boss is at his table. But rules differ from office to office and while some offices may be strict in this respect, others may do away with such formalities. The absence of formalities, however, should not do away with the form. Talking and speaking come next to gestures. A subordinate must learn to hold his tongue when the superior has taken over the discussion and unless he has to point out any outstanding misdirection, he had better be silent.

Employers

In the business and service world, superiors may very well be employers, but they are not always the same. A superior may be any one of the intermediaries who has the responsibility of managing or manning the office or a particular department. The employer, on the other hand, would commonly mean the highest or chief person in the organisation who has not only the power to give employment but also to relieve a person of the job, if need be. Employers, therefore, as a rule would not have any superiors unless, of course, we take into consideration all the customers and clients or members of the governmental authorities whom the employer has to be indirectly indebted, responsible or obliged.

The relationship between the employer and the employee should not be discordant. On the contrary, since a person has to employ or a person has to serve in one form or another, this relationship should be mature and sensible. It is a fact that if a person has to progress in his working life, he has to give his best to his employer. It is also true that an employer may get a number of persons in his employment but he may find difficulty in getting really efficient and devoted persons to work for him for any continued length of time. If that be so, the employer is just as much indebted to this loyal employee as the latter is to the employer. In short, workers there may be many and to spare but good and sincere workers are very few indeed.

If an employer considers his employee inferior, he would be committing a serious blunder. He pays his employee a salary in return for his work. He has to be considerate and kind to him. The employee cannot contribute his maximum to his work if he cannot rely on his employer at times of crises. They are the implements of production of wealth for the country. Only through cajoling and sympathy can the highest amount of efficiency be got out of them and that too with their cooperation. In a work-place where the employer is able to create the right type of cooperation and a feeling of mutual trust and friendship, the total efficiency may be automatically maximised.

It does not cost the employer anything to address the employees politely. The employer who generates in his employees strong bonds and works shoulder to shoulder with them may be permitted even to deal roughly with the latter who may take it since they may admire or worship their boss. *This boss has to be a moral master and not simply the physical or circumstantial one.* If the boss loses his temper, if he is inconsiderate, hard to please, revengeful and so on, he can never earn the respect of his employees. In the face of contingencies and chaos, it is the employer who has to take charge and command and lead his team. If, on the other hand, he raves and rants and is nervous and frantic, his employees will have scant respect for him. He is the employer, he is taking all the risks, he has to shoulder all the burden.

Colleagues

In an office, in reality, all persons are colleagues. The work is before them, they have to do their respective duties to deliver the goods jointly. The master and the servant, the superior and the subordinate may have bureaucratic differences but actually such differences are meaningless. As a colleague in the working force in an office, a person should treat another colleague with dignity and politeness. There is no room for snobbishness or for complexes. Noble birth, good education, possession of wealth have no value if a person is unable to perform the work allotted to him. His working efficiency is the first and foremost requirement in the office and he has to be respectful to all those who are engaged in bringing out efficiency in full to the surface.

Colleagues should not be placed on the same footing as friends. Certainly colleagues may become, in course of time, the greatest of friends but a behaviour proper to a friend may not be ordinarily proper to a colleague. Friends may be normally of the same age and status, but this is not the case with colleagues who may be of different ages and come from different strata of society. In the office if there is any difference, it may exist only in respect of work and nothing else. An elderly person has to show proper respect to a young person especially if the latter happens to be doing the same work as himself. Pride, aloofness and indifference are to be absolutely cast off among colleagues, or the work of the organisation will suffer. In proper co-existence and fellow-feeling, one should learn the art of working together with one's colleagues. The office is not the place for giving vent to one's emotions. People may laugh and talk and joke and even discuss family matters but work should get priority. As long as a colleague is capable, he is entitled to all the respect and attention, irrespective of other conditions such as his appearance, his status, his finances and so on.

Visitors

A visitor who walks into an office and expects a red-carpet treatment because of his position in the outside world may often meet with frustration and even humiliation. Every office has its own discipline and its code of conduct. The employer or the manager may be busy with an equally important guest or with a matter of grave concern for the organisation. It may not be possible for him to see the honoured visitor at once without previous notice. The visitor may have to sit outside, generally in the lounge or waiting-room provided for this purpose, but it quite possible in small offices that such a separate place has not been provided in which case the visitor may have to make the best use of a chair at the same table with an employee till the employer or the boss is free to call him inside.

During all this time the visitor's forte would be his smartness, wit and humour. If he frets and fumes, flushes and complains, he may lose his dignity and his mood. He has to be good-natured and find something to talk about with the employee during the period he has to wait. It is for the employee or employees, of course, to offer him some refreshment on behalf of the company and the employer, and be respectfully attentive without neglecting their own work. The more easily an honoured guest can adjust himself to a situation like this, the more secret or open appreciation he will command from the employees as well as from the employer.

It would also be bad manners for a visitor to turn everything topsyturvy in the office simply because he happens to come from a bigger concern or is a man of a higher status. A visitor has to fit himself into the structure of the office. If his ultimate objective is to see the chief of the office, he has to use his patience to get over the inconveniences that he may encounter, most of the time inflicted unintentionally. It is also not for him to ask questions or give suggestions or to be too persevering in pursuit of his objective. This of course has nothing to do with his business with the boss, but his dealings outside the boss's office, with the subordinates.

Visitor : I've an appointment with Mr K at ten.

Receptionist : May I have your card, Sir? (takes the card). I will inform Mr K. Please make yourself comfortable (pointing to the sitting arrangements in the room and indicating a seat to him).

Then after contacting the concerned person,

Receptionist : I am very sorry but something has suddenly come up. Mr K will be free in another five minutes. Could you please wait for a few minutes?

Visitor : Certainly, I'll wait, I quite understand.

Opposite Sex

In the age of women's lib, it is but natural that men and women should be working side by side in an office, in a factory and at other places of work. Gone are the days of the veil and prudery or false prestige. Women are now going ahead and clamouring for equal rights. While glamour and primness are attributed to the presence of women in the office, it would also be pertinent to mention that one would be mistaken to regard women in such places as only pieces of glamour or extravagance. These working women have their own capabilities and adroitness. The perfection of efficiency, that some of the women can reach in some professions or fields like positions of secretaries, receptionists and so on, may well be beyond the comprehension and power of achievement of many a male.

A male colleague, therefore, has to show adequate respect and appreciation for the work that is performed or attended to by the women-members of the staff. Women should be treated as equals. If a woman is doing a man-size job, she is entitled to receive a man-size treatment. It is true that in health, and physical strength a woman may not sometimes be able to match a man, but that has nothing to do with the quality of work that she is capable of turning out. It would also be wrong on the part of the women to find fault with their male colleagues and maintain fixed opinions about the male sex. It would not be right for women to keep to themselves in the office, or in their own groups. They should have the open-mindedness to work with their male colleagues congenially.

Kindness, sympathy, help, fellow-feeling are the attributes of the two sexes as colleagues in the work-place which may create the proper atmosphere of hard and continuous work. Notwithstanding the different capacities of the sexes, it should not be forgotten that a male member may be exhausted in the same manner as the female member at the end of a whole day's work and so in the spirit of camaraderie the small tiffs or the outbursts, if any, should be withstood by both the sexes. Any form of teasing, banters or unreasonable jokes should be made taboo in an office and unless the employees themselves consciously abandon such behaviour, the standard of the office may possibly suffer.

CHAPTER FIVE

Business

*I*n the business world efficiency is the key word. The businessman has to be all the time on his toes because complacency is hazardous. There are also some business ethics, and profit-making has to be resorted to within the framework and range of certain principles, otherwise an act of business may degenerate into a criminal action. Nobody expects a businessman to sell his wares at a loss. Also nobody would like him to have a windfall at the cost of his customers. That is why we have state laws almost everywhere to cut down the powers of the monopolist and bring him under control. Contribution to society should be the main aim of a businessman if he aims at winning in the buying-and-selling game.

Proprietor

It is not difficult to understand that the proprietor is the all-in-all in his own set-up. But this all-in-all terminology is a misnomer. A proprietor may puff and pound or beat his breast to prove that the business belongs to him, but he is not the omnipotent being in his concern. Without the cooperation and devotion of his workers and employees, he is a nonentity. He, therefore, has to get this cooperation from his men. He has to give them enough encouragement and incentive to love their work and the concern for which they are working. The most coveted treasure in a man is his self-respect. If proper dignity is shown to the employee, almost anything may be got done through him. In like manner, force, compulsion and command are resented. The polite proprietor can get his employees to do many more things at much less cost.

The ownership attitude of the proprietor is a hurdle to the advancement of his business. It is not the price of artistry or handicraft at which he has to work all by himself but it is something to be built up with the assistance of his employees, his customers, in fact, everybody connected with his business. If he tries to spread the feeling around that he is the sole architect, there is little possibility that his business will expand. People may shun him, his employees may hate him and he may have no goodwill at all. To save his business from such dire fate and consequences, the proprietor of a concern should behave like one of the employees of the concern working side by side with his workers, his helpers, encouraging and inspiring them as and when opportunity arrives. He may be in the field, yet not in a romping manner but in an obscure and unknown sort of way. He has to depend on his employees, forgetting the image of the one-man show. Such a theory in business is not tenable because no matter how efficient a man may be, he cannot go on expanding his business without able deputies and workmen. If he has to build up his business securely, he has to understand the proper relationship between employer and employee. He will do a great wrong if he chides or rebukes an employee in public. If any corrections are to be made at all, these are to be made in private and never before others. The employees must feel themselves identified with the concern and it is the employer who is responsible for encouraging their growth in this direction.

Chief of Organisation

It is needless to mention that the chief of the organisation is not necessarily the proprietor. In concerns with limited liabilities jointly held by different shareholders, the Managing Director, the Chairman of the Board of Directors, or the Manager may be endowed with the highest executive powers. There are different gradations of the chief, however, and persons like the sales manager, the agent or the branch manager may all possess maximum authority within their jurisdictions. The main responsibility in respect of etiquette that would rest on the shoulders of these persons is that of dealing with the outside world — the customers, the clients, the authorities, the public in general — in short, the maintenance of good public relations is their bounden duty.

A visitor enters an office and at once the attendant is all attention, helps him to take a seat and fetches an intermediary to cater to his needs. At another office, nobody is interested in him, nobody attends to him, a few of the employees he may get hold of may appear to be more interested in their own affairs than in anything else. The line of behaviour in the first office has been handed down from above with strict instructions as to how to uphold the honour, prestige and efficiency of the concern in the eyes of the public. The sharpness, competence, control and behaviour of the boss are apt to be reflected in the attitude of those placed at the lower rungs of the ladder. If the chief is rude, selfish, short-tempered, slothful or possibly inefficient, the people working under him may behave within the periphery of these undesirable traits.

The chief of the organisation has, therefore, to vindicate his claim as the main operative in the office. It is for him to lay down the rules of behaviour, to formulate and stick to them himself wholeheartedly and strictly. The chief who sermonises but does not himself follow his own preaching will be hardly taken seriously or obeyed willingly or properly. And this naturally leads to the question of his independence. He may rely on others for work but not for opinion. If he cannot encourage proper behaviour, the discipline of the office may be jeopardised. A superior should never be taken to task before his subordinates or the efficiency in general will suffer.

Business House Personnel

In a business organisation practically everybody counts. Starting from the very formulation of policy down to the minute details of implementation, completion, delivery and satisfaction, everybody is a wheel in the great machine. If there is any slackness anywhere, this big machine may go out of gear, and this may be measured only in terms of so much loss. All the personnel in the business concern are to recognise this responsibility and behave in a manner that is worthy of their role. They have to assist and advance, not fight and obstruct.

It is, therefore, necessary that these personnel should greet one another in the best way at the start of their day and also that they remain in good humour throughout the period they work with one another.

It is definitely bad manners to decry one's firm or concern before others, perpetually to grumble or complain and place all the blame on the company and the employers because they are getting the work from the workers in return for inadequate salaries. No self-respecting worker would indulge in this kind of vilification because it reflects on the worker's capability and shows him dissatisfied. There may be good and bad points in every job and it is the worker's duty to magnify the good points and minimise the faults. One thing is certain, and that is, almost everything is reported to the employer or he is not a competent employer at all and may be ousted easily by his competitors.

Further, an employee who falls into the habit of disparaging the employer would be wiping off whatever chances he may have of his own progress. As an employee goes higher along the ladder of success, he has to identify himself more and more with his concern. Simply by saying and feeling 'It is our concern', workers may help the company turn the corner for the best. Just as the employer has to train himself to look upon his workers as his own, so also the workers should grow in sincerely feeling for their employer and their organisation. When the workers speak well, the company is automatically upgraded and will leave the others behind.

Customers

No customer should take undue advantage from a businessman simply because he is a customer, but he is entitled to good and polite behaviour and all the attention that may be reasonably given to him. In this sense, a customer who may turn out to be an immediate buyer and a customer who may be only enquiring about a future purchase may be treated with equal courtesy. The enquirer may be a potential customer and if his curiosity is not whetted at this stage, a possible sale in the future may be lost. Many business houses, therefore, operate a counter or section to meet regular or stray enquiries because, if nothing else, it is a good means of having publicity and establishing goodwill.

The seller-customer relationship can be established only on a mature understanding and the businessman who feels personally involved in any bargaining or negotiations and allows himself to be carried away by his emotions had better take up a different vocation. The higgling-haggling over prices has nothing to do with personal insinuations and it is customary for a businessman to slide back to normalcy after a turbulent round of bargaining. The lawyers of the opposite sides compliment each other about the arguments, and greet one another after the contest, and so it goes on in every game. Business is also a game which is played by the seller and the buyer and like all other games, it has to be played in the spirit of a true sportsman.

The businessman, thus, has to keep two things separate, his personal feelings and the negotiation spirit. Especially in relation to his answers, he should not feel hurt if the bargaining-altercations are rather rough for him. Customers, on the other hand, should remember that because they profess to make the purchase they do not have the right to say anything and everything. It falls under shopping etiquette that when a buyer has entered a certain shop and has turned almost the whole stock topsyturvy, he should at least buy something, however small, by way of compensation for the time and energy of the shopkeeper wasted on him. Also customers should not forget that courtesy invites the greatest natural respect and hence no customer while buying a commodity should take it to be the last purchase from the individual or establishment. He is within his rights to bargain and examine but he should do these within the limits of decency.

The Counter-salesman: May I help you, Madam?

Customer: Do you have this shade of velvet?

Salesman: I think we do, please wait. He brings out one big roll of velvet. The colour is distinctly different. He tries one from a huge stack from a higher shelf and naturally things are disturbed, disarranged. The colour is almost matching, but not quite. He tries and tries and in the end has to offer his regrets.

Customer: I am sorry for causing you so much trouble.

Salesman: Not at all, Madam.

Customer: Please put this shade aside; if I don't get an exactly matching one, I'll take this.

It is, however, customary though not obligatory to buy something when the shopkeeper has been so keen to satisfy the customer.

Customer: Would you sell half a metre, by any chance?

Salesman: Yes, Madam, why not?

Customer: Then I would like to buy half a metre of this cotton print.

Others

The various types of persons who add to and enhance the prospects of a business cannot be easily categorised. There are the authorities, the public in general, the various intermediaries, like the commission agents, the wholesalers, the small shareholders, and those who may be directly or indirectly connected with the progress of the business concerned. Sometimes the interests of these people in the concern may be vague and insignificant, and it may be the duty of the businessman himself to consolidate these vague interests into sound propositions. It is through business etiquette alone that a business house may spread the sweet balm of its benevolence and utility to all and sundry who may happen to come in contact with the organisation.

In fact, the goodwill that a business organisation may be trying to build up through its various publicity media may be helped by the small attentions and even wee acts of congenial behaviour shown to everybody who is connected with the house. From the receptionist to the chief boss of the firm, the effort to please and satisfy has to be pursued. The telephone operator who has the first contact with a certain outside person has the responsibility to draw that person to the firm from this first conversation. If she is rude or careless or does not give the attention that may be called for, the first impression on the visitor or caller is not good, and very often it may be his first and last attempt to deal with the firm in question.

It may be a mistaken belief that a firm has to outsmart others by hook or by crook. Rather all the actions of the firm have to be above board. The saying 'cheat or be cheated' is actually not for the firm that purports to leave others behind. Overall respect cannot be accumulated all of a sudden by a single action, but by piece-meal deeds which have to be fool-proof in respect of duplicity, and this whole super-structure may tumble down through the short-sightedness of a few or even a single individual belonging to the concern.

CHAPTER SIX

Profession

*I*n any profession, the professional is mostly in an advantageous position, having to deal with novices, trainees, afflicted ones or those who are in trouble. The persons who approach a professional for expert advice may sometimes be absolutely at the mercy of the latter. It would depend on the professional himself to contribute his knowledge and handiwork in a manner that will provide the help-seeker to rescue himself from something or acquire for himself a part of the expertise with which he may carry on in his future life with grace and confidence. Professional etiquette is thus a must because the persons coming to him are all vulnerable and hence a professional is expected to maintain his own manners and etiquette unilaterally.

Professional

The lawyer has to know the truth from the accused or the defendant and try his best to save him from further shame and humiliation. The doctor has to be told about the symptoms and maladies of the patient to make him equipped properly to root out the ailment. The teacher, on the other hand, has to take full responsibility for the future of the student under his charge. Such experts can do or undo the fate of their wards. There is no denying the fact that for the professional, the fees that he charges may be the only means of livelihood. That does not mean that he has to be drained of the milk of human kindness or that he has to harden himself to such an extent as to make himself mechanical and turn himself into an automation.

The kindness and sympathy that a professional can bestow on his customer or client may remove the mental agony of the latter and restore his lost confidence. The will to fight is as necessary in the sufferer as in the benefactor. With confidence and normalcy regained, the client himself may assist the professional in making an invincible stand for him. The initial move, however, depends on the professional person who is taking up the case or the issue. He has to be gentle and attentive to his narrators of misery. If at all, he is to act automatically, he should be able to do it in respect of bringing out his feelings, and listening sympathetically because in the package assistance that he provides to the ill-fated, the human factor should be genuinely taken into account.

The ethics of the professional man should be clearly defined for him as well as for others who seek his help. A high and complete sense of dignity has to be maintained where clients, customers, patients or proteges are concerned. Their secrets are his own secrets, their welfare is his own welfare, their improvements are to be watched and followed with parental care and affection. It is not what he contributes but how he does it that is important. If the doctor laughs at the pains of the patient, the lawyer jibes at the crime of the accused, the tennis or the sports coach loses his temper because of the inefficiency of the trainee, there will be hardly any solace for the incompetent, any hope for those who have made mistakes and are striving to overcome them.

Client

Granting that the professional-client relationship is mutual, there is also a code of conduct for clients. This code may not vary much from manners that the students have to assume in dealing with their teachers. The client, customer, patient or anybody who is seeking professional assistance from another person has to have complete faith and dedication to that person. Doubts and disbeliefs have to be abandoned. Even if the professional tries his best to bring relief to the aggrieved party, the former will delay the process of advancement if he remains passive. If he is satisfied with the authenticity or bonafides of the man from whom he is to receive expertise, he should no longer entertain contradictions or confusions about the latter. He has to be open and straightforward.

Duping the professional person from whom help is sought, by way of lying to him or hiding facts from him, or misrepresenting facts and incidents, can only slow down the process of success for the customer. The customer in this case is not just any human being to the professional man who has taken charge of him but he is a case, a sort of symbol, some matter, or an item that has to be turned this way and that, experimented with in every possible way to arrive at best results. Patience and faith are, therefore, the twin virtues of the person who is seeking moral or other help. Similarly, envy, jealousy, revenge are the worst offshoots of imbalance and no client, customer, patient, or student should cultivate such feelings. The teacher or the doctor may not have time for individual attention for each student or patient in the way it may be wished by the student or patient. Only with understanding will the receiver have the chance to get the most and best out of the former. One who receives justice is equally blessed along with the giver and the customer in this case certainly is such a blessed one.

Intermediary

There is a whole host of agents, go-betweens and others who become instrumental in the meeting between the professional man and his customer. These go-betweens are not always mercenary persons and may, more often than not, be prompted by humane considerations. In the professional world, these persons are sometimes invaluable and even indispensable, because through them the down-and-out person may get in touch with the most competent man in the line. The professional should not decry the intermediary nor should the client shake him off as somebody superfluous or unwanted. On their part, these intermediaries are not to forget their own self-respect. If they play one principal against another to gain monetary benefits, they may lose their name and foothold in the field. They have to be in the clear and the advice that they give has to be genuine and effective.

Those who succeed in the working world as intermediaries may forget themselves as such for the slur, that the layman may sometimes cast on them unknowingly. They may pursue their vocation with ardour and straightforwardness with the sole aim of benefiting the community whom they serve.

Just as in the business world every single person counts, so also in the professional field everybody connected with the trade or deal commands his or her importance. Cooperation and fellow-feeling should be present all along the line from the professional himself to his customer and then onward to everybody who has a small or big say in the matter. The professional who establishes this team-spirit in and among the whole retinue of persons who are connected with his profession would naturally be regarded as more enlightened than another who is ignorant and this goes for the intermediaries as well on whom lies the burden of increasing the prestige of the calling.

Fellow Professional

The other professionals in the field are competitors no doubt but in their dealings with one another, the feeling of antagonism should be substituted by the bond of fraternity. Free and fair competition is to be applauded but deprecating others in the same profession and pointing out their faults to belittle them are to be eschewed. The client or the customer may have preference for one adviser in place of another. This personal preference has to be accepted and acknowledged by a fellow professional with tolerance and in good grace.

Etiquette in the professional field requires that all the professionals should work for the total good of society. They must help the development and extension of their science. Their performance has to be heightened to the maximum. Their skill or expertise has to be perfected. There is hardly any scope for competition or mud-slinging here. Politeness, sincerity and spirit of coexistence towards one another in the same profession should be unquestioned and prevail always. Errors and genuine mistakes cannot be avoided but it is better to have a fair and open discussion before accepting another's customer. Professional unity and integrity have to be preserved at all costs at all times.

Thus, there is more scope for consultation in professions than for outright competition. The professional who knows his limitations and sticks to thoroughness within his limited sphere is apt to be popular and will prosper within that circle. All fellow-professionals are equally in need of assistance from one another. There should be no rancour, no remorse, only the will for better performance and general betterment. For that reason, between the lowest and the highest in the profession, snobbery has no place. If professionals view their work as business, they may be mistaken, because they are not buyers and sellers of commodities but their work refers to services which are concerned with human welfare.

Fellowmen

Professionals are, after all, human beings in societies, and apart from their colleagues and customers, there is the whole range of people who surround them, with whom they have to coexist and communicate socially. The professionals' attitude to all these people is important because, besides professional efficiency which may be confined to the court, the clinic or the college, they have to give something of themselves to the world. They are human beings essentially and in mixing with their fellowmen, it would be better if they could mix with them on an equal footing and not as experts or superiors.

Also, it cannot be denied that they may be superior to many but this superiority they must never allow to surface. Professionals are the guides, path-finders, social workers, some sort of preceptors, and they have to maintain this dignity and live up to this expectation. What is more, they would blunder if they equate themselves with the common lot. They have to lead the latter, assist them, advise them for self-improvement, even though they are not rendering such help in their professional capacity. False insinuations should not touch them. Rather, it is they who may be called upon to quell such conflicts between others, just as they would spend their energy in thwarting those directed against themselves.

If this is true, then in their behaviour with their neighbours and fellowmen these experts are not to hammer in their differences. Nor would it be right for them to take it for granted that they are accepted automatically. They have to prove themselves as human beings and give expression to their human character to prove to themselves as well as to their fellow beings that they are not mechanised robots but humans possessed of all the qualities of head and heart.

Conversation outside the courtroom between two opposing lawyers:

First lawyer: I daresay you've got a good stand now with the new plea you've taken, provided it is accepted.

Second lawyer: I don't see why it shouldn't be. Your junior lawyer is a rough element, though. Why don't you talk to him some time? He almost shouted into my face today.

First lawyer: Young blood, but don't you worry, he'll come round. Well, so long now.

Second lawyer: See you in court tomorrow.

Conversation between husband and wife:

Wife: Darling, would you mind putting off the light, I'm sleepy.

Husband: Sure darling, just this one page to this chapter or would you that I had rather stop?

Wife: Oh, have it your way, but only this one page, mind you!

CHAPTER SEVEN

Correspondence

*C*orrespondence has many advantages. What cannot be said may be conveyed in writing. Some unpleasant truths can be driven home through the written word, if this is at all necessary. Why do written words carry such weight? There may be more than one reason for it. The receiver of the communication firstly can read the contents over and over again. Secondly, he may also take it to be concluding proof and may thus be more than satisfied. Thirdly, written words do have the power of magnifying the sense whose import on the reader may be more lasting. Another reason that cannot be overlooked is that written words go to form literature where reason and the imaginative faculty combine to produce good writing. Good writing has a better power to impress than if the same thing had been spoken.

Official

Official correspondence bears the stamp of great responsibility which may be easily understood. This responsibility pertains to the fact that an official letter may travel to any authority up and down the ladder of bureaucracy and that action may be taken on the same at the lowest and highest levels. Apart from the fact that official correspondence has to observe all the etiquette of address and approach, it has also to be careful about the contents, accusations, stress, avowals, admissions and so on and so forth. When a correspondence is issued officially, the originating source should be prepared for action taken on it, either favourable or unfavourable, backed even by the ultimate authority, if the requirement be such.

Clarity and brevity are the necessary ingredients of official correspondence. Paragraphs must be devoted to single points mainly, or at best to allied matters. The beginning and the end must be pleasing and should convey politeness and form. Economy of words is to be observed, though a certain form of ornamentation at times may be necessary. It has to be remembered that each word in an official letter carries much weight and may be variously interpreted. The writer, therefore, should be careful about the possible significances of words and expressions used in the communication.

Disputes and disagreements are thus the by-products of an official correspondence and the issuing source has to take care of all the pros and cons before the communication is despatched. Quickness and pointedness are the virtues usually associated with official correspondence. Haste in reply should be abjured, or corrections or amendments may have to follow simultaneously. Clarity of vision and the spirit of reconciliation, of give-and-take, are the ancillaries that help to solve the matter, and give the needed solution more readily.

Business

Sometimes the distinction between business and official letters is slight. The major distinction between the two types is that while the commitments in official letters may be regarded as final and irrevocable, the same in a business letter may not be so final due to the Bilateral character at the back of such correspondence. bilateral agreements may be overlooked if the interested parties so desire, while a rule of authority or of the State may not be overlooked. Business letters also may or may not be precise, depending on the stage of correspondence. If a new party is approached, one has to write at length in order to impress the other side about its capability. Once, however, replies are exchanged, the communication should stick more and more to the essentials.

The main objective of business correspondence is to produce and preserve business, and to take negotiations to their successful end. Business correspondence, therefore, has to take care of both form and mood. To understand and reciprocate the underlying sense in the correspondence is the first step in business manners. It is politeness to express refusal in mild terms and this refers to the proposal stage when acceptance or postponement is communicated. The clear negation, if there be any, however, has to be used in orders, offers, cancellations, etc., and in final deals. In the business world, the importance of something or somebody may ebb and flow like the tide. The correspondence that does not leave scope for retrieving or retracing steps or reopening closed matters lacks the fundamental principle of business formalities. And hence the business letter has to be constructed on a non-committal basis, as far as possible. If no such possibility is foreseen at that moment, there is no harm in putting in those very words, hinting that future probability may not be hoped for.

The mood of the letter is important because the party that catches the mood rightly may also be able to secure the business. The taints of refusals or disagreements may be traced in some lack that has produced dissatisfaction somewhere in the negotiation and sometimes an alternative proposal of an increase in the number of choices may find its mark even in the face of a negative reply. Whatever the reply is, whether favourable or unfavourable, it has to be sent expeditiously and even a letter of thanks where no business has been contracted may create a good impression on the other party to be encashed in future. In this connection reminders or follow-up communications may be helpful but reminders have their own tone and procedure and, if carried to extremes, they may prove counterproductive. Reminders have to be especially soothing in language and since they constitute straining the etiquette, they ought to be humble and understanding. This kind of follow-up action should pay special attention to maintaining reasonable gaps between the chasers.

Personal

It would be wrong to suppose that personal letters do not have any form at all. The success of a personal letter would be evident where the personal note is clearly brought out. There may also be some nominal etiquette which if followed may add glory and colour to personal correspondence. The first of these relates to extra-personal or intellectual references and jottings which not only make a letter boring but may even miss the point sought to be made. Right from the 'address' down to every detail and to the ending, a personal letter should bear the imprint and character of the writer. It may be obligatory on the writer of such a letter to bring the written language down to the simplicity of a conversational talk, where formalities and framework are shed to bring the writer and the reader closest to each other. This would be coveted excellence in such writing.

Equality is the keynote of etiquette in such correspondence. It may be regarded as an established fact that many personal letters, lengthy, advisory or flowery, are not read properly or thoroughly because of the aversion of the reader for the writer. Such an aversion can be surmounted even if that very writer tries his hand at not simply writing but winning over the reader, not sermonising but making an attempt to sound interesting and to arrest his attention. Among the 'don'ts' in the personal letters, the 'do-this-and-don't-do-this' manner has to be completely discarded and substituted by suggestions and possibilities. This is more effective because the writer in showing respect to the addressee also evokes the latter's respect for him, and a mutual feeling of understanding is generated. A personal letter that is incapable of arousing such warmth in the other party fails in its mission and since it is curt and dry, it may run the risk of only a cursory glance by the recipient, with much of it remaining uncommunicated.

Written words have the capacity to soothe out knots in relationship. Even the most disagreeable matter can be brought home through mild and sympathetic language. It must not be lost sight of that words may be effective both ways and just as an agreeable expression is appreciated and remembered, so also a disconcerting implication or an outright blame may affect and keep alive a long-lasting animosity. The etiquette to be followed in this is that it is better to leave things unsaid than to pour out one's venom and grievances because just as an arrow, once shot, cannot be taken back, so also words written in haste may go on creating trouble forever.

Rank and Nobility

It is imperative to show deference to rank and nobility. A judge, a cabinet minister, a governor and a maharaja or a king command respect because of their responsible positions in society. They evoke the trust and acclaim of the public and the State with regard to their positions. Communication with high ranks and the nobility must be formal and is generally carried out in the third person. Kings and queens are addressed as Your Majesty and referred to as His Majesty, Her Majesty or Their Majesties. The Prime Minister and other Cabinet Ministers are addressed as Your Excellencies and this is the form of address for any ambassador of either the home country or foreign countries. A judge of a court or high court is spoken of as Mr Justice So-and-So and is addressed as Your Lordship, while a Bishop is The Right Reverend— the Bishop of—

These forms of addressing are used in letters and a minister or an ambassador is to be addressed as 'Your Excellency' in place of 'Dear Sir' at the beginning of the letter. At the conclusion of the letter in place of 'Thanking you', 'With kind regards' or 'With kind assurances', expressions like 'I remain Your Excellency with assurances of the highest obligation or consideration' are to be used. In the body of such letters, it is customary to use 'Your Excellency' or 'Your Excellency's' wherever 'you' or 'your' appears, but to avoid redundancy, the form may be a little streamlined and in-between the lines apart from the beginning and the end a simple 'you' or 'your' may be used.

The officers of the Armed Forces — Army, Navy and Air Force retain their ranks permanently, and a Commander or Air Commodore has to be addressed and referred to as such. When a subordinate is writing to a senior officer, the former may address the latter as 'Respected Sir' but where acquaintance is deeper and the subordinate is known to the boss well, a form of address like 'Mr Gordon, Sir' or 'Mr Tuteja, Sir' may be appropriate. It may be mentioned in this connection that this form of address is also to be used by a subordinate when he is informing a superior officer about some matter in a room where the latter is talking or conferring with others, or when the subordinate is compelled to get an officer out of the group to attend to some business matter that requires his immediate attention.

Formal

Formal occasions naturally call for a formal response. State invitations, even some invitations of major importance in the private circle, may need a note of formal acceptance or non-acceptance. Sometimes the invitations may not require a formal acceptance, in which case regrets for inability to attend may be communicated in time. Formal correspondence in such cases should be in the form 'Mr and Mrs So-and-So thank Mr and Mrs X for their invitation but regret their inability to attend the dinner due to indisposition/previous engagement' and so on. However, it may be mentioned that the importance of the occasion, that of the person inviting and of the one invited are to be taken into account. The precedence and priority of one occasion in relation to another cannot be denied. Thus a funeral may have precedence over a marriage which may be found more important than other engagements.

If there are two persons who are sending out invitations for the same date, the choice would be on the invitee, but if one person is socially and officially superior, it may be tactful not to quote the other engagement as an excuse for not accepting. Where the person invited is superior in status to both the inviters, the option may be with the invitee to attend one occasion and send regrets to another. Short letters despatched after a ceremony thanking the hosts may sometimes be optional and may depend on the taste and proclivity of the person concerned. But an after-dinner (or any invitation) note may be obligatory from the etiquette point of view where the invitee feels it to be a favour for being invited and where he would like to perpetuate good relations with the host.

The characteristic of a formal note is that it tends to maintain the relationship at something other than the personal level. In official contacts and discourses, formal responses cannot be done away with. But some formal relationship may mature into personal intimacy in which case rigid formalities may be slackened. There are, nevertheless, cases where such a possibility may never arise like an invitation from a government department or from a high executive's office. In such instances, the third person should be used to avoid any personal touch and the language should stay within the limits of official etiquette.

CHAPTER EIGHT

Marriage

*T*he sacred institution of marriage is preserved by active roles in participation and protection by the husband and the wife and also those who consider themselves well-wishers of the family. Notwithstanding the religious mores and the moral precepts ingrained in any marriage, the everlasting happiness of the couple is a result of conscious effort for understanding between the marriage partners. The blending of two human souls, however attuned they may have been or suited to each other, is a fragile affair unless the renewals of trust, love, mutual assistance and even dependence are carried on all the time. It is necessary for the wedded couple not only to be civil to each other but to build up their devotion to truth, justice and equality. The words 'and they lived happily ever after' with which a majority of stories usually conclude to have a joyous ending, in fact, start the process at the very beginning, which is to culminate in the whole of married life. The real trouble may start when either the husband or the wife takes the other for granted. The range of etiquette that takes in its fold the full vista of married life should depict primarily the various ways in which the husband should act to give his wife chances of maximum fulfilment and *vice versa*.

Husband

The wife is not a chattel or a personal property that can be dealt with in any manner desired. The wife is a human being and a partner without whose contribution married life may well prove a failure. It is not the maintenance of the wife alone nor meeting her daily and occasional needs that may suffice for the wife's mental growth and contentment. Gifts and ornaments may meet the need for a time but would hardly create a permanent base. It is the little acts of kindness, the small tokens of devotion, the off-hand commitments of acceptance and coexistence that count most and keep the female partner happily preoccupied.

Firstly, the etiquette of treating each other courteously and with respect is among the musts. Secondly, mental compatibility is essential. Whenever it is possible, the two partners should supplement and complement each other to achieve the greatest harmony for the family. No work is demarcated as such, and wherever there is a gap and necessity, one should help the other according to need. The husband is the pace-setter since he is the head of the family and any initial moves is to be expected from his side. If he is well-equipped in this art, he would know how to impart training to his wife without offending her.

Offences are hardly forgotten. They may disappear from the mind for the time being but at dark moments of married life, in the face of tiffs and disagreements, they come to the surface and appear with redoubled ugliness. The husband is physically the stronger partner but married life cannot be equated with a dominated existence because issues are formed by tiny sentiments and pile up to make the concrete block of happiness or calamity. The husband's show of strength in the marital sphere is evident in his patience, endurance and understanding. His calmness and purposefulness would annexe to the family the crown of dignity, hope and ambition, aiding the husband and wife to encounter the pitfalls of life.

Mere show of affection is not enough and no matter how artificially with perfect etiquette the husband and wife behave before others, it is they themselves that would count in the ultimate analysis. The real offence committed against the family and the wife, in particular, is the neglect that the average male may be blunt enough to allow to seep into the relationship. The family ties may grow more and more tenuous and fragile. if this lapse is not remedied in time. Care and attention are the best gifts a husband can give his wife and in his married life, he cannot afford to omif these. To give respectful treatment before outsiders or in public is the first and foremost etiquette. Also, to love his wife is the duty of a husband and no mature husband would find it below his dignity to show affection to his wife before others.

Wife

The housewife's job is a full-time occupation. If the husband has the responsibility of maintaining the household, the wife has the duty of preserving the same. The first few years of marriage may be said to be years of adjustment. This is also the period for the wife to learn to accept the situation of the be-all and end-all of affairs she is to manage. The husband, young as he may be, may return from work to enjoy the pleasure of the wife's company. This is the time for mutual give-and-take and to plan for a better tomorrow. If the wife harps on the pressures of her own day and her worries she thereby upsets the mood, and giving of oneself to mutual blessedness and happiness may disappear.

A well-groomed appearance and a hearty greeting of welcome may be all that a husband may require to boost his spirits and start the evening on an ebullient note. The vestige of this novelty has to go on during the early days of marriage until a deep-seated trust is firmly implanted in the minds of both the spouses. The business of dinner itself has to be a bit of a piece of art. Whatever lack of comfort there may be in this, whether regarding food items or the mode of preparation, the evening has to be made pleasant by personal attention, care, smiles and a great deal of charm. It may sound preposterous but in the early years of marriage, too much may be expected of the wife and what the wife may do is to live up to that in the best way she can, remembering that it may be a passing phase for the husband, who at this initial period may expect from his wife some magic to turn his home into a mini paradise.

Bedroom manners count most in these early years of marriage because here, as nowhere else, the husband and wife have to face all the intimacies of their living and small rubbings of nerves in the wrong way, tiny discords, a few false steps, etc., may appear magnified to one of the partners or to both. The husband may like to have the light on for some bed-time reading or he may like to take a shower or exercise before turning in or he may like to smoke cigarettes, one too many. The wife may also take an unduly long time in finishing her chores, she may not care for much grooming at night, her tastes may be too refined or too average and so a secret war is on — the war of nerves. This can be avoided if the wife, who is in charge of the home, and has much time in those first few years to think and plan, understands easily the needs of the husband. With a little intelligence and tact, she can make a success of her marriage.

In-Laws

As modern couples are becoming more and more liberated they prefer to live apart from their parents. Education and enlightenment are bringing about this change in India. Sophisticated land reforms and the breaking up of the joint-family is also a cause attributable to it. The in-laws can contribute greatly to the attainment of bliss and concord in married life. They are the blood relations of both the spouses and as the saying goes, 'blood is thicker than water'. It is painful to cut oneself off completely from one's near and dear ones. But married life is an organisation that has to be cultivated and as a unit of society, it has to ward off any threats that may disrupt its peace. If the in-laws are unreasonable and adamant, there may be no other course left for the saving of the marriage than getting separated from them.

The husband's parents and other cognates are generally the most proximate ones to the couple. The bride has to leave her own people and stay in a family most of whose members may be and often are strangers to her. It is the duty of the in-laws to take the bride within the family circle. She is not a stranger or a visitor in the family and everybody in the husband's house including the servants may be made to realise this. Sometimes the brothers or sisters of the husband may create problems. This is quite understandable since the young may be led more often by the heart than the head. But the older members of the family have to bring them together through adequate briefing and admonitions, if necessary.

It is not outward behaviour but inward response that counts most. Insinuations and innuendoes tend to make the relationship strained and bitter. Acceptance or rejection may be evident through little gestures or small talk. It is not always possible for the husband and wife to come from the same economic background or the same social class or status (as long as we are not living in a classless society) and a clash of cultures may not be entirely avoidable. If the elders in the family are sympathetic and take pains unobtrusively to train the bride (since the bridegroom has generally less contacts with his in-laws), the dark clouds of misunderstanding may not form at all. Just as the new bride is expected to try her best to be one with the husband's family, so also the members of the husband's family have to extend their helping hand on all occasions to make the bride adapt herself to the new family in a natural and gracious way.

Friends

Friends are essential to married life. There are, however, different categories of friends, some of whom may be quite intimate, while others may be just acquaintances. The young couple may find it very interesting to entertain and be entertained. This is important for them to get their first lessons in social discourse and contact. The choice of friends, however, is significant because for couples and newly married people, lasting friendships come from those who are also married. It means that the most mutually satisfying friendship for a newly married couple would be with another newly or recently married couple. If, on the contrary, a newly married couple acquires the friendship of another young couple with quite a few children, the mutual benefits may be one-sided or reduced to nil.

Since friendships are of various categories, the closest friends need to be of similar dispositions and responsibilities but there may be no harm in having acquaintances with different family backgrounds. Rather, a variety of experiences in between regular life may prepare the couple for things to come and lead them to take on more responsibility in the future. Bachelor or single friends of newly-married couples should have the consideration that the former's way of life could not now tally with the latter's. These friends should have the good sense to restrain themselves and their demands on the couple.

Real friends of the couple would turn out to be those who would have the consideration as to when to leave them alone and when to expect their hospitality. It may be difficult for the newly wedded to withstand everybody who does not belong to their own kind or to their set. Other friends who are not so privileged should not feel envy on this account nor seek to barge in at inconvenient hours or force their company on the couple unduly.

They may remember that everybody has his place in society and these somewhat distant or not-too-close friends may also have their functions in giving training to the couple in formal social behaviour, while the closest friends may enjoy intense relationship whose usefulness may get over in a few years' time.

Vocation

Marriage is best worked out on the foundations of love and work. When love culminates in marriage, theory passes into the stage of practicality. It is through joint endeavour and elation in each other's success that married life attains its desired end in the worldly sense. In the first few years the married couple may need reassurances from their partners *inter se* more than when they become more mature and get somewhat settled in their life and suited to each other. The interchange of love and loyalty at this stage has to assume both active and passive functions: active in the sense that to speed, goad and guide the other partner would be just as necessary as passive acceptance and reciprocity of feelings. This, however, calls for much tolerance and stamina in both the partners and generally love and strong attachment provide the sense and judgement when mature reasoning may be lacking. It may be sometimes necessary for the young husband to talk about his office, his boss, his colleagues, his efficiency to the wife at dinner or at other intimate moments. It is equally expected of the wife to talk of laundry, crockery or curtains when the young man's head is full of sales promotion ideas. The diverse currents meet somewhere and that is how two young people may shape their marriage nest, depending solely on the spirit of toleration, appreciation and encouragement, despite the fact that they lack the experience of their elders.

Where the husband and wife are both working, they have to make adjustments with regard to each other's work. The wife may be a teacher and the husband may be an engineer. Both of them may bring home things to study and correct and unless each gets into the habit of showing respect or importance for the other's work conflict may easily arise. On the contrary, it may sound astounding how personal support or a stand-by attitude by one may help the other get ahead with his work. Thus the husband and wife may help each other in their work, though their vocations and work have nothing in common. Where the work is the same and they are more or less colleagues like two professors, scientists, doctors, lawyers, a greater spirit of accommodation may be needed. Here, personal feelings, individualistic ideas, superiority and inferiority complexes and other sentiments in case of competitors have to be played down. If the husband thinks that it is he who should be ahead, he is committing the greatest blunder and where the wife is endowed with better gifts, the husband has simply to accept this fact. What is more, he should give all the encouragement and support to his wife. By this he is not making any sacrifice, he is only cutting down his ego to desirable size.

The terms equality and equitableness are good milestones in the household of working spouses. Equality is by all means a noble word but a more justifiable one is equitableness. It would be impractical to think of equality where the two married partners have different capabilities. At the same time, they may settle down to concede to each other equitable values on the basis of each other's performance and significance. No watertight compartments are possible in this and a wife is entitled to equitable and equal treatment even if she has not much material practicableness. It is when the family vocations join hands and the husband and wife strive for higher and higher attainments individually and together under the fostering care of each other that the married couple's competence is the highest.

Hobbies

Work and pleasure, togetherness and separation comprise the course of the full cycle and life is apt to slide down to monotony. Hobbies provide an escape from such a bottleneck and in a newly married life where enjoyment and interest are to be kept alive, where the success of a marriage may be directly proportional to the amount of accomplishment in this direction, hobbies are good media to help the couple move from one new interest to another. There is the cultivation of new hobbies as well as the nurturing of old ones. The new hobbies may draw the interest of the couple jointly. The woman may paint, write, be fond of gardening or house plants, keep pets and so on. The man may frequent sports fields, read and try his hand at do-it-yourself jobs.

To pursue a hobby in married life has its merits and demerits. The thing about a hobby is, it may grow and grow and claim every moment of a person's spare time. This may be true of both husband and wife. To help either of the married partners not to get so involved and entangled as to neglect the other, hobbies have to be tackled properly, so that they do not become too time consuming or demanding. Nevertheless the etiquette regarding this has also to bear the theme of encouragement and indulgence. There is to be mutual assistance in each other's hobbies, as far as possible. It is, indeed, delightful if one of the partners can be co-opted to pursue the hobby of the other, like the wife's taste for gardening may be passed on to the husband and so on. In such a situation both the husband and the wife can then enjoy the same recreation.

In the early days or years of marriage, it may be difficult for either of the partners to follow his or her hobby, much less allow the other to devote time to such pursuits. This is but natural because of the intense need for the blending of the two personalities and to get such a blending may be more pleasurable and more realistic if each married partner is allowed to retain some of his individuality from the beginning. Moments of absence and separation may make the union more refreshing and binding and they may thereby learn to value the other more objectively and realistically, so that no extraordinarily high expectations may be entertained about each other.

Associations

*T*he social aspect of human existence is of great importance in the different groups and associations that an individual is connected with. Though grouping is not a very admirable quality, a person who is unable to mix in different groups may be said to have some shortcomings. There are different societies suitable for different individuals, bachelors, unmarried people and married couples. The advantages to be derived from such associations are many. Firstly, they inculcate in the members a sense of group-spirit and belonging. The latter in its way leads to security and a feeling of reassurance. A person who is a loner may be a genius but if he lives in seclusion, much of his time may be taken up in explaining to others that he is not different from them. Another merit of association is that cooperative and community welfare work may be taken up and implemented for the benefit of all.

Clubs

Clubs exist mostly as recreational institutions and the members should devote themselves to the very purpose for which they exist. If it is a dramatic or cultural club, a place for cards and indoor games or a sports and outdoor games club, the members have to propagate the purpose of the club. In other words, to join a club and then not to participate in its activities or to go on criticising it for this and that deficiency is the height of bad manners and even of misbehaviour. There are reading clubs where the members are expected to read, ladies' clubs where the members may be all females (though there is no harm in the attendants being males) as well as there are hiking clubs, gliding clubs, smokers' clubs and clubs for various other purposes and ideas.

Members may choose to be either active or remain passive. The latter would like to follow the crowd, be one with it and do whatever duties may be allotted to them from time to time. Active or passive, members render their full support to the policy of the club and the decisions of the management committee are seldom disputed or called into question. However, not all clubs may have such a smooth sailing and their failure may be attributed to some extent to the non-cooperation of members. If the members lose track of the main ideals and get involved in the policies of club managements, or if they break up into too many factions or groups, all with separate ideas or themes for the club's welfare, none of the groups may acquire enough power to implement their coveted plans. Club-spirit is against groupism. If required, the offending or obstructing members may be asked to leave or resign.

Club etiquette would require that the members mix freely and on an equal footing with one another. They are not to take personal matters to their club and bother other members with their worries or problems. Club life is different from home life and though a few members may discuss some personal or business matters, essentially business life and club life are to be kept severely separate. Easy though it may seem, the performance requires some practice for the novice or the uninitiated. Mixing and relaxation are the twin objectives of club life. This mixing, however, is to be differentiated from social mixing, and it is quite possible that a person may have one set of friends socially and another set of friends at the club, and the twain may never meet. The efficiency of a successful club-member is to keep the two separate.

Societies

The purpose of a club is mainly to provide relaxation, enjoyment, diversion, etc., while a society may come into being for a particular purpose and it may continue to exist as long as that purpose is present. Thus, the society for prevention of cruelty to animals may find its existence meaningless if Government regulations are passed to safeguard all kinds of animals in the same way as this society would like to go about it to protect animals from human neglect or brutality. In the same manner prohibition societies may cease functioning if drinking is declared illegal. The society to aid flood victims may still exist even after the victims are provided help and rehabilitated. Such a society may take up some other allied objectives to keep itself occupied.

It is needless to say that just like the club a society may have its constitution, its rules and regulations providing for disciplinary action against its erring members. Some societies are actually clubs like a dramatic society or a debating society, while societies like the cooperative credit society, employees society, house-building society, etc., are organisational groups existing for the discharge of certain responsibilities or for the implementation of certain objects or ideals. The membership of a society is mostly voluntary and is generally optional in character, though there may be compulsory societies like a parent-teacher society in certain schools, or residential welfare societies in a locality where membership is compulsory by virtue of an incumbent being either a parent or a teacher or owner/resident of the locality, respectively.

It is expected of members that they behave in a mature way and discharge their part of duties in small and big ways. It general meetings are called, members should find time to attend them. If help in cash and kind is required, members may do their best to contribute. If other duties are needed to be shouldered, the same may be taken up without much ado. Trust and respect among members are necessary. The feeling of hurt, grievance or complaint has to be eschewed. The purpose and objectives of such societies are not to be forgotten in the form and formalities, in the different sittings and ceremonies that may be held. Sincerity and sacrifice in members are called for because most of these societies are voluntary welfare bodies. It may not be forgotten by members that pomp and splendour are secondary, that if a charity show is held in a posh theatre or a fashion show in a five-star hotel, the functions are a means to an end, and they are intended to benefit the needy. In these cases involvement in the via-media should not be the only criterion or consideration.

Organisation

Any association with some kind of management may be considered an organisation. The manners that are required of the different members of the association would be the same as those required in the organisation itself. The only difference is that in an organisation the nature of participation may be stronger, so that voluntary or compulsory differences may vanish and in their place, ordinary, normal and honorary membership or filling up of priorities may be the rule. This would mean that organisational responsibilities may be more binding.

When a person is a member of one or more organisations or is on the management committee, he has to devote himself seriously to his work. In most cases, the work may refer to social work of all kinds and grades but sometimes cultural, sports or other kinds of activities may be taken up, but even in these cases, the idea of service to the community forms the core of action. Group envy, personal jealousy, temptations and hankering after power in the set-up and allied things are vices that mar the very purpose of an organisation. These things may crop up because of the largeness of the body. One who is not public-spirited or is conditioned to the necessity of community welfare would do better to steer clear of these associations. But once one is involved, there are no two ways in which one should act. If one finds oneself lacking in capacity, time or sincerity, one should withdraw or step down and let a more competent person fill the position. There is grace and honesty in this.

Work brings fulfilment, and belonging to a known and big organisation apart from one's own vocation develops the various sides of a man's character. One may become an adept in mixing with different types of persons. One loses one's self-consciousness and in trying to do good, one brings out simultaneously the good that is in oneself. In other words, one fulfils oneself. Latent qualities are brought to the surface. Confidence and assurance are increased. The social existence of a person is openly manifested. As one advances in this direction, one learns to behave appropriately in the social world.

Mixed Groups

Mixing may be homogeneous or heterogeneous. In the latter case, since the opposite sexes are brought together and in close proximity, they learn the art of co-existing with one another. Simple co-existence, however, is to be distinguished from proper mixing. This is because in the former case, in an association or organisation, the gents and ladies sections may be separate and segregated, and they may not come in close contact with one another except in times of some general functions or ceremonies. This type of side-by-side existence has no proper meaning from the etiquette point of view except that one should stay away and should not be in the way of the other section's activities.

A true mixing of the sexes may be called for in some married couples' clubs or some associations where men and women work hand-in-hand for the fulfilment of their mission. The first of these etiquettes would refer to the awareness of the other. It would be the height of bad manners if a person is so self-conscious, shy or snobbish that he or she is indifferent to a member of the opposite sex or that act may be tantamount to such indifference. If awareness is maintained and properly applied, two members of the opposite sex may talk pleasantly in the spirit of two members of equal status. The important thing to remember in this is that there ought to be no purposefulness in such discourses. These talks or casual meetings may take place for a few moments when the male and female members may simply smile and nod at one another at landings, at entrances or elsewhere, or they may stand on the sprawling lawns of the club premises on a winter afternoon and discuss various topics for hours together. Similarly, men and women out on a social camp job may be cramped or huddled together in a van or a compartment and spend a dreary hour or two or half a day by enlivening the occasion with conversation, jokes and snacks.

A prolonged mixing of this type may create in a person, male or female, the ability to mix, firstly, for the sake of mixing and, secondly, to let sympathy and the helping attitude ooze out of his very being. It is when companionship or friendliness is established between the opposite sexes without any demands that the experience of belonging to mixed groups may be said to have matured. There is no particular way a person should behave in front of a member of the opposite sex of the same group except that the concerned behaviour has to be within the bounds of reason and decency. The sense of decency, however, varies from group to group and as long as basic good behaviour is maintained, obscenities and abuses are eliminated, the pattern of mixing may be some what relaxed or totally disciplined.

CORRECT MANNERS AND ETIQUETTE

Voluntary

The voluntary nature of clubs and associations distinguishes them from workplaces where one is bound to carry out one's duty and to remain in one's job. It has to be admitted that this absence of compulsion turns association jobs into enjoyable recreational activity. A person who is interested in rendering services for a cause may become a member of the association. The action that is forthcoming for voluntary membership is generally prompted by the member's inclination and willingness to give himself to such actions. The member concerned, however, should not take voluntary duties lightly. We may remember that even if the lightest of duties is not carried out properly due to carelessness or inattention, the result will be that the easiest of actions may be badly done or not done at all. Voluntary or compulsory, any action that has to be performed would deserve to be performed well with one's whole-hearted concentration.

The main duty, therefore, of voluntary workers is to take their work seriously and give the best account of themselves in the field without a supervisor. In voluntary action, there is little or no scope for indifference or neglect. The incumbent has to assume full responsibility. He has also to keep all sides of his nature under control. His anger, irritation, impatience, inconsideration, etc., have to be folded up as long as he works voluntarily. Also, it would be bad manners to feel superior about one's position. Because a person is working voluntarily, it does not mean that he can do anything and everything according to his whims. A rich man may be distributing food or clothing to the poor. He cannot get cross at the eagerness and indiscipline of those who have come to receive help. If another person is offering nursing help to others, he has to make himself stand the misery, dirt and uncleanliness of the diseased persons if they happen to be destitutes. Again, snobbishness and selfishness do not go with voluntary work. If any person accepts voluntary work because that has been the fashion, he or she may not be sincere to himself. Unless one acquires the spirit of service, it is futile to take up the work just to please others or flatter one's own ego.

Recreational

From one point of view, recreational manners may be more rigid than those used in offices or elsewhere. Since the need for interchange of deals or business may be absent in recreational activities, the simple etiquette that one person has to show to another cannot be omitted. It would be bad manners for one to disturb the feeling of relaxation or recreation by bringing in subjects or topics that would invariably cause some disruption to the smooth enjoyment of leisure by another. Sometimes even talking would appear to be intolerable, and if a person has to keep to the manners of such a situation, he has to learn to respect the feelings of another person for quiet pleasure.

Another thing that recreational manners require is that where everyone is relaxing, it is improper to be formal in clothes or behaviour. When the party is on the beach a person wishing to join it should be in beach wear. Similarly, where every person is casually dressed and is letting himself enjoy one another's company, it would be foolish not to be able to catch the mood and remain apart while still physically present. It would also be wrong to take up sermonising while out for relaxation in a group. Debates or discussions, which may kill the spirit of relaxation, even if enjoyed by the persons concerned and may affect the fun of other, should not be encouraged. Sometimes the behaviour necessary for a relaxing attitude is to be able to maintain one's silence. It is said 'silence is eloquence'. More sense and thoughts may be conveyed to the other party if the parties know how to stop and when and where to stop talking.

The art of relaxation or recreation is not so easy to master and a person has to have quite some experience in this field before he can achieve confidence that he would be a good sport in a relaxing group or a recreational party. The most important of the qualities which is required is to talk and to keep silent in turns. When the feeling of relaxation goes deep down the systems of the persons who have given themselves up to this pleasure, their actions and inactions may come almost spontaneously from all the persons in the group. After lolling about in the sun for some time and doing or saying nothing to each other, all the members of the group may suddenly come to the decision of playing some game or doing something to activate their limbs. If all the members of the group have been relaxing seriously all this time, they would all feel the same urge and with the exception of a few, the new activity or sport may be taken up with general enthusiasm.

It may be repeated once again that the art of relaxing is to be learned through experience and discipline. If a person has his thoughts all the time, pertaining to matters of money, politics, writing, or his job, or some forms of material pleasures, it may be really difficult for him to give himself up completely to the pleasures of relaxing. There are, however, big executives and important personalities who though burdened with grave matters of concern may know how to give rest to their brains and their bodies. May be the art of relaxation should be a part of executive training.

Public Relations

Public relations happen to be a wide term and may mean all types of contacts with the outside world or circle. Just as the public relations section in an organisation may cater to the needs of publicity and other media to popularise the name and goodwill of the company, so also at home public relations would give a certain family or household the opportunity to boost its standing in the locality where it is residing. The first requisite of public relations is that the image of the person, body or organisation has to be properly projected in the sphere where public relations are being valued and taken up seriously. To get this done in the best possible manner, it is necessary that everybody connected with public relations is fully briefed. If the person giving information hesitates or expresses his doubts or is not sure or is ambiguous, the whole effect of public relations may be lost or neutralised.

To have a trained staff for public relations, therefore, is very important. This training has to be rounded up by adequate briefing, so that all the persons disseminating news, facts and information may spell out the same thing and may not be contradictory in their expositions. Politeness is the next requisite of the public relations department. The spirit of help must be inculcated in the persons engaged in this work. If boredom or indifference or impatience and absence of calmness and gentleness become evident, the persons seeking information may drop out forever and the company, organisation or society may lose the support of people. What is more, the dissatisfaction of a few may be communicated to many, and the organisation gets a bad name for a small lapse on the part of the telephone operator who had replied curtly or some member of the staff who had been unwilling to help. The incidents may be insignificant but they proclaim the inefficiency and bad management of the concern. This is because one employee may be inefficient or careless but if the company values discipline, it would train all its employees to behave courteously according to a common code of conduct. Can we ever imagine a soldier not to obey commands and still be in service without getting the prescribed punishment for inefficiency?

At home or at work, public relations have their place. The good name of an office is necessary for its progress. The good name of family gives a prop to children in their growing up by providing a background of respectability and honour. It is a wrong notion that show of strength is proof of power. Humility has the power to keep hidden a far greater power than can be imagined. In humility and modesty, in good moral character and normal behaviour may lie the true seed of courage and grit, a courage that is indomitable and all-pervading. Public relations thus are a major part of public and private life. Unity is strength, the dictator is a freak, the individualist is indeed a recluse. One can go ahead suppressing others, but not for long. Real advancement occurs only with the acknowledgement, acceptance and acquiescence of all.

CHAPTER TEN

Dinner

*D*im lights, soft music, whisperings and movements, rustle of silk, the coiffure, the perfume — a dinner always gives rise to such snippets. The waiters, the mild hustling, the set and laid table, the settling down, the confidence and correctness of manners, the laughter and lightness of spirits are also accompaniments of a dinner. The banquet with its over-sized table, liveried waiters, high-backed chairs, complete with toasts and music lays claim to etiquette as the *a la carte* dinner at a restaurant or the cosy foursome at a residential dining-room. A dinner is not very different from a luncheon or tea or any other kind of party where food is served. What makes a dinner outstanding among these is the blend of relaxation, formality and friendship that seeks to culminate in a mellow acquaintanceship, bringing two hearts closer than in any other engagement. Such harmony may not be possible during the harsh reality of the day.

'What would you like to have?'
'Whatever you are drinking.'

A conversation like this between the host and the guest may be quite in order in a place where drinking is allowed and accepted. And given below is a scene at the beginning of a dinner:

Mrs Richter joined them, and a moment later a comfortable grey woman — her hair, uniform, and even her skin were the clean, muted grey of a rain-filled cloud — Emma, announced dinner. They crossed the hall and went through the inviting 'other room' and into the dining-room. The mellow mahogany, twinkling crystal, flickering candlelight, smooth linen, and handsome silver were a reflection of Mrs Richter's perfect taste ... 'Will you sit here, Bob?' Mrs Richter said, motioning to a chair on her right. (From *Two Souls, One Body* by J. Marks and H. Phillips).

Formal

At a formal dinner, every aspect tends to conform to certain norms. The invitations which are usually printed cards (though letters of invitation may also be despatched) have to be sent out to invitees well before time to avoid last-minute refusals and regrets. These, however, cannot be avoided and every hostess or host has to be prepared for a few last-minute cancellations. The next on the card in a formal dinner is the dress, and if nothing is mentioned to the contrary, evening dress (as is in vogue) is to be worn by men and women.

Formal dinners on most occasions are given in honour of some dignitary or important person and it is customary to invite persons of the same rank and calling or same status to have a homogeneous group at table. Avoid very young guests if the majority of invitees are somewhat older and also for the maintenance of a balance between the number of male and female guests. While bachelors are invited alone, single ladies are invited along with parents. If it is a small dinner party, a single bachelor-guest may feel a little awkward and to balance that one or two other bachelors may be invited. Since all the burden of making these preparations falls on the host and hostess and has to be undertaken in advance, regrets to attend a dinner have to be tendered sufficiently in advance. A host or hostess who do not have some acquaintances and who do not mind attending a dinner at short notice may have to face embarrassment due to last-minute cancellations.

A formal dinner is mainly a sit-down dinner, though at small dinners drinks before dinner may be served in the sitting-room. Soft drinks may be served in place of hard drinks and the conversation may be light and short. Grouping of any manner and talking only to one's neighbours are to be discouraged. In its place, the conversation had better revolve round a general subject and should include as many guests as possible or at least those within hearing distance. Some conversational gifts are necessary for a successful dinner-party conversation. Discussing one topic after another serial-wise may make a dinner party highly boring. On the other hand, conversation that proceeds spontaneously and freely, one topic or situation leading to another, is more enjoyable as it taxes nobody's brain. The hostess has to keep on talking in turns with guests, making them feel at home.

The service at the table as well as the placing of crockery and cutlery (knives, forks, spoons, etc.,) on it is important. There are quite a few arrangements in this. If the dishes served are such as may require either knife-fork or the spoon-fork combination, knives, forks and spoons as alternative arrangements may all be placed on the table. The soup-spoon which is the largest is placed either on the right or on the space above the plate. Whether on the right or above, it has to be the most outside item of cutlery. Other items of cutlery are to be arranged according to the dishes served, from outside to inside and the spoons, the topmost and lowermost, respectively, in that order. It is not good to have too many knives and forks on the table and a reasonable arrangement in this has to be arrived at. The serving is done from the left beginning generally with the right-hand guest of the hostess who is to sit at one end of the table with the host at the other end. It is bad manners to eat with one's mouth open and all chewing is to be done with the mouth closed. When using knife and fork (or spoon), elbows on both sides should not be raised unduly but should be reasonably pressed to one's sides. One has to be careful of one's movements. Upsetting a glass or letting a knife or a spoon fall may cause embarrassment to everybody present.

Informal

Invitation cards may or may not be sent in the case of informal dinners. If cards are sent, the word 'informal' is mentioned below, at the left-or right-hand corner. This word may mean quite a few things. Firstly, it refers to dress. The dress is to be informal. That is to say, the invitees may wear whatever they like but the host and the hostess believe that the guest's preference will not be something too obvious or too out of fashion. In summer, in a climate like India's, the dress may be a 'bushshirt'

126

and in winter a lounge-suit for men. Secondly, it may eventually turn out to be a sit-down dinner with serving by servants and all, or it may be a buffet dinner where everyone helps himself, or both. The courses of food, the manner of serving also may not conform to any definite form.

Informal dinners may be arranged first by contacting a prospective invitee over the phone and finding out whether he or she would be available either singly or with spouse for the dinner engagement on the tentative date. If a particular person is not available for that date, then another person may be contacted, and so on till the person giving the dinner is able to arrive at the requisite number. After that, cards or invitation letters may be sent to them. Informal dinners are more in the nature of get-together parties for getting acquainted with new people. They stand in between a small party and a formal dinner. The conversation also should flow along lines of relaxed discussion and formalities are done away with to make mixing and talking a delightful experience. Certainly, informal dinners may be sit-down affairs as well, in which case some form of seating is to be maintained and it is better if serving could be done by an attendant. Some hosts or hostesses would like to have formal dinners because, though it is true that formal dinners require more attention to details, they are in a way easier to manage than informal dinners.

In an informal dinner, however, there is no known range of informality for the host as well as the guests. Moreover, if by any chance one of the guests fails to read the direction on the invitation card and appears in full formal dress, the fun of the dinner party may be subdued.

Private

If you are having a private dinner, it may be formal or informal, but it may lack the strict formalities of an official dinner. In an official dinner, generally, there are speeches, toasts, etc., and to most official dinners which may be in honour of visiting foreign teams or delegations, the males or officials (who may be women) are invited. The main point of the private dinner is the home-like atmosphere that has to be generated to provide assurances to the invitees that it is merely a recreational event, whatever the form. The hostess has to play a great part because in private dinners, it is the hostess to whom the major share of the responsibility would go. She has to see to the convenience of the guests, their preferences for different kinds of food, their tastes and idiosyncrasies. The host also may not remain inactive and should render all possible assistance to his wife or mother or sister and to perform this act of help without being conspicuous.

If a note of anxiety or worry as to how things would go persists at a dinner, it is apt to spoil the evening. In a private dinner, there should be no show of anxiety at all. This should be a time for smiles and merriment, and even if something goes wrong, it should be faced in a humorous or joyous spirit. This goes for the guests as well. It may very well be imagined how things would shape if the electricity suddenly fails in the midst of a dinner. The hostess may rise calmly and inconspicuously, light candles kept in the cupboard or on the sideboard and while she or the servants are at this job, somebody at the table should start some joke like 'I am fishing out pearls like a diver' and hold some piece of food with the fork. Or, somebody may remark 'Oh, good, now we're in space. You know what they say about the colour of space, it's absolutely violet, would you believe it?' and so on and so forth. The height of bad manners would be to say nothing and wait and keep quiet till the candles are brought in. And when the candles are brought in lit, of course, there is that remark, 'Ah, perfect! A real candle-light supper, and you know what happened the other day when we had been to a moonlight picnic ...'

It would be evident from this that at private dinners people should feel free and make others feel likewise. There are some private dinners given by stiff-necked persons to some exclusive group where the behaviour may conform to some norm. Many a tale is strewn with such dinners held by the rich, old or aged ladies whose fixed habits and manners are nightmares to the young, and also how some non-conformist young man or girl would say or do something to upset their apple-cart. Leaving such cases aside, the guests and the host and the hostess in a private dinner should try to come close to one another, as far as possible, under the circumstances. Jokes may be essential but not of the type one would enjoy at picnics or other very informal gatherings. Also, depending on the group itself, the nature of conversation should be on knowledgeable subjects.

Intimate

The intimate dinner has to be very exclusive in the sense that the circle for an intimate dinner has to be closer than that of a private dinner. The modes and manners to be followed at such a dinner are not set and may vary from person to person, or group to group. The main objective of giving such a dinner is to enjoy intimacy with the persons invited. The official, formal and even private dinners cannot fall under this category because these lack that touch of intimacy which is so essential. Intimate dinners may be for two or more persons and the manners and etiquette to be followed on this occasion are more in respect of the conversation that accompanies the dinner than anything else. Maximum fellow-feeling has to be evoked and the host as well as the guest or guests have to have the reassurance that they are in need of. The friendly and congenial scene which highlights a dinner that may be called intimate lends it a very personal touch.

One may talk about everything at such a dinner but it should be of mutual interest. Stories and jokes may be important parts of it but such things have to rotate round the interests of those taking part in a dinner like this. Personal achievements and experiences, so far as they depict the relationship and concern of the others taking part in this dinner, may be tolerated. It has to be kept in mind that official and artificial talk or even social conversation may be redundant at such dinners where the host and the majority of the guests invited may like to talk about something else. Thus, old cousins may invite each other once in a while or periodically to reminisce about bygone days when they were kids. Talk about the past and about one's glorious youth may leave them flushed with the radiance of sweet memories. To talk about something else would break the magic spell of this rare occasion of deep intimacy.

It is also true that everyone does not like to live in the past and as such they would be rather poor guests at a dinner which is meant to be a sort of trip down memory lane. A man of the world may not be able to adjust himself to these sentimental displays. Nevertheless, if at all, he attends a dinner of this type that is given solely for the purpose of reviving old memories, he should also try to move with the crowd and get himself involved, as much as possible. If he feels himself to be far removed from such things, he may not attend such a dinner on some excuse. Intimate dinners are also given to deepen and consolidate the relationships and feelings between the host and the guests. A free and sincere behaviour is what is needed at such dinners, where there is pleasure in attending, and joy and thrill in inviting. The oneness of mind is the main criterion, the confluence or sameness of purpose is the guiding factor and, lastly, the unison of views and attitudes is the clinching or cementing medium.

Family Reunion

There are in every family some occasions when family reunions do occur and at most of these times such events are enjoyed with great relish. One distinguishing characteristic of a family reunion is that the participants are mainly blood relations and so the initial barrier that separates other types of hosts and guests may be absent. Of course, there may be cases where the members of the family have stayed away too long from the family, so that family ties have almost come to be severed or are already severed, so much so, that these members have nothing in common with the older generation. In such a case, it may be difficult to accommodate and include these members in the family in the same way as other members, but still if the wish and the inclinations are there on both sides, their getting into the family stream may not be difficult or awkward, after all.

This inclusion in the family-flow and the ability to get into the situation is what is important for all members of the family who may be visiting the family regularly or are just sporadically dropping in. All these members have to fit themselves in the family system and the dinner which they may be attending may thus turn out to be a very happy affair as well as hilarious, rollicking with fun and merriment. Status and symbol are to be forgotten and one must be able to give one self up to the enjoyment of another's company. One's tastes and tendencies are to be curbed to give priority to those of the family and if one has become unaccustomed to their ways due to long absences, one may always try one's best to learn and acquire the requisite taste. The children, especially, who may be under different tutelages consistent with the different segments of the family, should be made to behave properly and taught to respect the family tradition. If this respect and love for the family are missing, there is no point in attending such reunions.

Similarly, in the case of food and table manners, there has to be the spirit of give-and-take and since the children or the young naturally look up to their elders, it would be the responsibility of the older people to behave correctly and direct their children properly. If the feeling of superiority or inferiority persists or there is some bad blood or feeling of some old feud between the members, the family reunion may be spoiled indeed, but since in a family reunion dinner, it may not be possible to include some and exclude others, in case of diverse trends and tendencies or animosities, frivolous or strong, all these have to be subdued to give prominence to the family spirit. Talk that may touch on some weak points is to be avoided at all costs and general discussions should be resorted to, as far as possible.

Buffet Dinner

At these dinners, there may or may not be attendants. Before the dinner starts, drinks may be served in the sitting-room or elsewhere by the servants and with this generally light snacks are also provided. Where hard drinks are served, the host or the hostess has to remember that these have to be somewhat in the nature of appetisers only and, therefore, the flow of drinks may have to be controlled, so that the guest may not be tempted to over-drink and misbehave. Strong drinks, where these are served, help to loosen the tongue and to brighten the atmosphere. Step by step the guests may open up and talk and laugh with others without constraints or complexes. Once the talk starts, it would be the duty of the host to let the talk and discussions move on and rise to a crescendo. When sufficient time has passed to give the guests a feeling of relaxation, the guests may be led to the buffet table.

If there is enough space in the house where a separate dining-room could be provided for this purpose, the guests can be led from the drawing-room to the dining-room. Where the dining-room and the drawing-room are combined, food may be brought with the assistance of some helper or servant and arranged on the table. It is, however, better for a buffet dinner to have the buffet table not exactly in the drawing-room but in some adjacent room or covered verandah, where food can be served on to plates and brought back into the drawing-room to sit and eat. The plates, the cutlery, the napkins are all to be arranged neatly on the table and the guests are to help themselves to food. Sometimes an attendant or hostess may be there to hand these to the guests one by one.

The buffet is a type of informal dinner and the people joining such a dinner have to lend their cooperation to the fullest extent. They have to have charming manners in getting the food themselves and eating with ease, poise and grace since they have to hold the plate in one hand and do the eating with the other. In taking food from the table, one has to keep in mind that there are others standing behind and hence one has to be quick and at the same time steady and confident. There is a particular type of easy movement which one has to follow, so that movements, round the table are smooth, easy and orderly.

The buffet is essentially a community or cooperative affair and as such consideration for others should play a much greater part here than in any other dinner. It would be bad manners to heap one's plate with food in one helping. Rather, it is within the buffet-dinner etiquette to make use of at least two or even three or more helpings to avoid the piling of food on one's plate. Since the guests will have to eat holding the plate in one hand and eating with the other, there should be more chairs placed here and there all round the place. This is particularly necessary because though some of the guests may like to come back to the drawing-room, others may wish to sit somewhere where they would not have to worry about spoiling the carpet or the sofas.

CHAPTER ELEVEN

Luncheon

*L*uncheon which is a mid-day event is also generally a somewhat quick affair since the host and the guests may both have to attend to their other duties just after it. For this reason, even though the time allowed for this occasion may be sufficient, there is always the sense of hurry with which a luncheon meet has to be concluded. The official luncheon, at the end of which serious matters may again be taken up and disposed of, or binding agreements may be contracted, may impart much gravity to the occasion. Except for family or friendly lunches and that too on holidays when a feeling of relaxation is there, most of the lunches are semi-official affairs. The one important merit of a luncheon meet is that almost anybody and everybody may be invited to it and even strangers may get together and have a nice lunch and then go on to their respective duties and hence, while a dinner may give rise to a reciprocating obligation, a lunch may not always do so.

Business

It is customary in business circles to invite the other party to a lunch and this is normally returned by a counter-lunch by the other side, provided the other side has the time and are not just roving negotiators. The main etiquette in a business lunch would revolve round the conversation at table. Though there may not always be need for all members to talk, the talk that may follow may be about some business matters or light enquiries and discussions about the place, city or country, but it should not be directly about the business on hand. Business lunches may be sit-down affairs since these are held at hotels and other eating-places; or these may also be buffet lunches arranged again at hotels or at such other places. The etiquette at a lunch of this kind is to talk without giving oneself away, to be friendly and sincere without confiding.

There are various kinds of business relationships and contacts and the behaviour in conformity with these to the respective lunches would also be somewhat different. Thus there is one type of behaviour when two parties are contacting each other for the first time, another type when the deal is under consideration, yet a third when it is completed. There may be no end to these degrees of relationship and the most difficult of these may be the situation where both the parties have come to a stalemate in their discussions and some breakthrough is sought to salvage the deal but is not yet arrived at. In such a situation, both sides are adamant and may not agree to budge from their bargaining positions.

All these different situations are to be cemented at the luncheon table and to keep to one's best manners and etiquette on such occasions would require tact and a sporting spirit, the two rival cricket teams going for lunch, one side on the point of victory and the other side on the verge of defeat. The tact and art manifested in high level business or official lunches are part and parcel of the business acumen of the executive or the official taking part in the lunch. It is to be noted that this kind of lunch has to be perfect and herein lies its greatest utility, that is, to let the other party realise that in spite of conflicting interests, there is no real hiatus or enmity; on the contrary, there is goodwill and sincerity on both sides. It may also be certain that the party that will play its hand better to the satisfaction of the other may gain one point over the other and the deal, if concluded or opened, may be to some extent in favour of the better-behaved counterpart.

In some official luncheons, speeches are in vogue. The host or the person who is hosting the lunch on behalf of some organisation has to deliver some sort of address and should request the chief of the other side (when the luncheon is in honour of some delegation or visiting foreign team) to say something by way of conclusion. If it is a big lunch pertaining to a conference or a seminar where the big hall is filled with long lines of tables and chairs for lunch, there may be any number of speeches before the toast, with some drink in hand, is proposed by the person who is selected to preside over the luncheon. A delegate to such a conference or congress should be prepared with a ready-made speech. Though the onus of speech-making is on the leaders of different delegations, all members should have a few words to say by way of thanks and so on.

Private

Private lunches and dinners are almost similar in principle though the extent of response to the two different events may differ.

139

While at a dinner the association is closed, it being the final engagement of the day, at a lunch that finality is absent. The day is not yet over and there may still be many things requiring the attention of both the host and the guest or guests. Again a private lunch may be as small an affair as a lunch for two, while every dinner worth the name should be at least for a foursome. As for conversation, that may or may not be allowed in a private lunch, there is no restriction as such and when two persons are lunching all by themselves, they may talk of anything that may please them, even filling time totally with business talk.

If business and pleasure are to be kept apart, why is it that two men thinking and talking about business should eat together? Will it not hamper or stand in the way of their relishing the food? Not necessarily. The fact that two persons have come close to each other regarding some business matters may prompt the two business negotiators to have each other in a more relaxed and easy mood. If a great business sense is required while coming to a solution at the conference or the negotiating table, a far greater tact and mixing power may be called for. Experienced businessmen at such times would talk of small things and narrate anecdotes to keep the minds of each other off the main business, and in this both the sides should aid and abet one another to pass lunch-time successfully and without any hitch. Those who are inexperienced in these matters may take this kind of occasion to get close to one another and they may talk of all personal and intimate things and may even appeal to the other side in order to clinch the deal in their favour. In such a case, the inexperienced party would be at a disadvantage in respect of the other who is more experienced and while the former would have all the chances of placing himself at the mercy of the latter, to all intents and purposes, the latter would have the possibility of having a better hand in this deal.

Private lunches, however, retain some sort of a formal character, in which event, invitation cards are issued to the invitees. If, however, sometimes the time is short to inform guests or to send cards, the host may just telephone and directly contact the guest, conveying his regrets in not being able to send the card in time. As for dress, at a private lunch there should be no restrictions regarding dress which may be what the guest is normally wearing or is supposed to wear in the season. But if the invitation allows sufficient time for giving an intimation to the invitee, then the latter may use his discretion and put on normal office-wear at lunch. If it is a hotel lunch with the hotel having a certain standing like a five-star hotel and so on and if there is enough time to have the lunch-information beforehand, the invitee is expected to go in the office-wear which in winter in a country like India may be a lounge suit, and in summer may vary from a safari-suit to the shirt-trouser-tie ensemble.

Residential

Lunches that are held at residences may have a deeper significance and importance than the ones held at hotels or other public places. This is because a luncheon being a semi-official event would need extra care if it is to be held at a residence, while it could easily have been held at a place outside which facilitates the holding of such ceremonies. But if a lunch is arranged at the house of the host himself, it would naturally mean that the host is giving more importance to the guest and is trying to render an extra favour to him. The hostess has to take part in this lunch and that would show that the host would like to have the relationship with the guest on a more intimate and personal basis and not merely on the official or business level. Sometimes, of course, if the guests are only a few, the host may give some excuse for the absence of the hostess and the hostess may stay in the background if she so wishes.

A buffet lunch may be held at a residence but if the guests are not many in number and if the servants are available at the house, it is better to hold a sit-down lunch because it would save time for talks that the host must have intended to hold. This is, thus, another reason why a lunch may be held at a residence. It is so done because the host may like to have both things together and keep the negotiation less open than if it were held at the conference room of the office. At a residence, all hurry or haste could be eliminated to a large extent; and it is quite possible that the host may take the rest of the day off from office to carry on with lunch and the talks that are expected to follow it. At the same time, the person or persons who would be attending such a lunch may have come from another city or town and consequently may have more time on hand than another who is staying and attending office in the same city. If there is no hurry, the lunch may proceed in the same manner as a dinner with all the leisure and luxury of a post-prandial repose.

On such occasions, the talks would naturally centre round the business that the parties would like to get done interspersed with titbits or other light conversation that may be thought necessary. Since the intention is clear on both sides, it would be expected that the parties would talk and do all the negotiating during the lunch-hour and also afterwards. However, it is a matter of courtesy that the actual business talk may not be introduced or raised until the luncheon is over and until the guest sits in a relaxed mood to start the business talk in right earnest. In such cases, the chief men may do well to have along with them some deputies if need be for assistance in the talks.

Friendly

A lunch that is held among friends would naturally have to be on a holiday when there is ample opportunity for friends to enjoy their leisure. A friendly lunch may be arranged on a working day but since the working day restrictions like return to work and so on cannot be dispensed with, the spirit of a 'get-together' may not fully receive free play. A friendly lunch is free from any formalities, it is true, and yet there are different degrees of friendship and different stages of the same. Moreover, the friendliness in adults is different from that in those who are young and tender in age. The adult world of friendship cannot do away with duties and cares that are there for them to face. A day with friends among adults should not normally cross the limits of the restrictions imposed by having to take care of one's family and the nearest ones.

The hilarity and the boisterousness that may be expressed at such a lunch have to be in conformity with the friends' positions and ages. The older the age of the lunch party members, the calmer may be the tone of enjoyment, while there is practically no specification for such a party held for the very young people. But even then these very young people should be taught party etiquette and they should behave in a manner marked with more gravity than what is required in their day-to-day mixing. Coming to an adult lunch party, it is a general rule of etiquette that one should not tease or criticise or be scornful in one's behaviour to one's friends in such a party, no matter how superior one may be to one's companions. Unless worldliness in this sense can be got rid of, the lunch party cannot acquire a true friendly character.

Usual rules of conversation are also applicable. One should not talk and go on talking about oneself, one's family, one's job and one's achievements. Conversation should be shared equally by all invitees. If the guests (or one of them) tend to be inconsiderate, it would fall on the host or the hostess to moderate the lunch-room conversation, so that nobody in the party feels left out. At the same time, it would be bad manners to cut short a speaker before he or she has finished, simply because time is over. It is also permissible to cut jokes since the party happens to be among friends, but here there will have to be limits and the jokes that are suitable for young people may not be so for those who are mature and aged.

Festive

Festive or community lunches may be held on a number of occasions. To commemorate something, a festival or even just a bigger sort of get-together may be held. Some clubs and colonies do organise things like these which are always on a big or even a mass scale, and the whole garden or place like that may be a riot of colour with the costumes of the invitees who are going about their affairs as it suits them. At such a party the responsibility of the host or hostess is much less and though it is the duty of both to mix freely with the guests and bring them together as much as possible, it is hardly probable that the actions and behaviour of all the guests can be controlled in such a large gathering.

Generally, these parties are informal in nature and the one thing that the guests are to bear in mind is that they should cause no disruption nor eat or drink to excess, so that they may require the assistance of some sort and may give rise to some commotion. The behaviour pattern for guests at such a party should not break the rules of natural conduct and all types of grouping, seclusion or intimacies that would exclude others are better avoided. Also, one should not keep aloof or be indifferent so as to become conspicuous. On the other hand, every guest should try to make a go at mixing with whoever comes along and be ready to join in the conversation of the group in which he may be included for the time being.

It is necessary for the guest to meet the host and the hostess at the earliest opportunity, in case he has arrived late and the host or the hostess is not at the entrance or at any noticeable place for the purpose of reception. Meeting the host and the hostess on arrival and at the time of departure is essential at such big gatherings where such slips may easily occur if a person suddenly leaves with one party or another. Also it is customary for young persons at such a lunch to make themselves of use to the host or the hostess and to render some help or be ready for the same if occasion arises. For the older generation also, the rule is to speak to as many guests as may come their way and to take keen interest in fellow-guests while conversing with them. They would be a drag on the party, on the contrary, if they only sit at one place and do nothing to take part in the get-together.

Party Lunch

A coffee or morning party may lead to a luncheon, which the hostess may arrange impromptu without much preparation. Certainly not all the guests may be able to attend such an on-the-spot lunch because they may have other engagements. However, a friendly party may sometimes naturally lead to a lunch by the same host and hostess and those without other appointments may stay on. These guests should at once realise that a lunch is a more serious event than an ordinary or snack party since the host and the hostess are offering a major meal of the day and no matter how simple it may be, it would require more thorough arrangements.

The switch from an ordinary party to a lunch party has to be attended by guests with some etiquette that would make the lunch party, however inostensible it may be, a success. The first thing is personal cleanliness. Since the lunch is a bigger affair, the guests may retire and have a wash and make themselves more presentable after the sweat and heat and enjoyment of the earlier party. A hostess is always pleased to meet neat and tidy people at her lunch-table. If would be the duty of the guests to take the lunch party not as an extension of the party they had attended but something new and fresh. They should, therefore, prepare themselves to take part in this lunch party.

This change-over from one party to another will naturally mean a different set of manners for the same guests and the talk and conversation or jokes, if at all, have to be on a subdued note. It is subdued in the sense that the note of the previous party cannot be continued in the lunch-room or while taking food and the guests have to bring out their lunch-time manners. Thus a new party is on the anvil and it may again be shaped according to the taste and inclinations of those participating in it. Sometimes when the guests and the host are equally adept in this art, they may bring themselves to talking on something quite different which may be suitable for a group of persons who are eating their food and little by little another party may be in full swing calling for different manners and actions.

Thus, it is like a change from one dance to another. The change from participation in one party to participation in another in the same premises or by the same host will have separate starts and finishes. In a morning party in which the guests had been participating, the guests and the hosts may come to behave very informally almost to the point of extracting enjoyment at the cost of one another since it is a friendly party and for their own enjoyment. At a lunch party, however, this attitude of carefree individualism has to be curbed and in its place cooperation, politeness and mutual help will have to be generated. It is quite possible that while in the morning party one guest has deprived another of the last snack and the act had created amusement all-round, the same thing when done at a lunch party would appear to be the height of impoliteness and bad manners.

CHAPTER TWELVE

Reception

olour and gaiety at a reception may be on a grand scale. There are social and religious ceremonies which require that invitations should be sent out to many because these are to an extent formal matters, and as many as possible should be accommodated. Receptions are, therefore, big gatherings where meeting and exchanging goodwill are of greater importance than anything else. At a dinner party, every guest has to be served well so that he or she can have a full share of the meal, but not so at a reception. Certainly the guests are to be offered snacks and drinks (soft, strong, hot or cold) but the stress is more on the meeting itself and celebrating the occasion than on food. This attitude is maintained both by the guest and the host and it is common knowledge that looking after the guests at a reception is easier than at other types of functions like a lunch or dinner.

General Reception

Organisation at a general reception is more important. The host or the hostess cannot see to the comforts of all the guests and so the host has to enlist the help of kinsmen or paid attendants. Even then the supervision had better be in the hands of somebody close to the host or somebody whom the host may trust. The attendants have to serve snacks and drinks in a polite and orderly manner.

No attendant should push or touch the guests. Attendants have to be there and at the same time their presence should not be conspicuous. Talk, conversation or quarrel among these attendants would lessen the prestige of the reception. These paid attendants should render service for the money's worth, moving and serving silently and staying in the background, as far as possible. The art of supervision at the same time would consist in having the whole reception under perfect control with an extra eye for the needs of the guest. A guest may be in need of plain water or a light for his cigarette or he may like to put down his empty glass somewhere. It would be a great relief to him if somebody looks after all these needs, somebody whom he may approach for his minor problem, or if a waiter appears at the right time at his elbow with a tray for collecting empty glasses.

It is generally the rule that the host and the hostess should stand at the entrance of the place where the reception is to be held and this is where they should normally welcome the guests. However, some other persons may be placed at the gate to bring the guests to the host and hostess who may be standing or sitting at some place inside. At receptions, guests generally stand and talk though there may be sitting arrangements and those of the guests who feel tired may sit down. However, going to a reception and at once sitting down and staying put all the time is not expected of guests and even where people are mostly taking seats, the new arrivals should stand on their feet sufficiently long before sitting down.

It has been pointed out already that, contrary to a lunch and dinner, a reception is not for satisfying the appetite. In line with this, the guests should not grab food and drinks and should take what is reasonable or proper. Also to go without any food or drink at a reception may not be good manners, and a glass or some food should be in the hands of the guests to give the picture of congenial and comfortable participation as one takes an overall view of the reception. It is also bad manners to monopolise the host by engaging him in some important or binding matter which the host is unable to break away from.

Cocktails

Cocktails generally are more homely affairs than receptions. It is needless to say that in cocktails, wines and spirits may be served along with other soft and cold drinks. Snacks are also provided at cocktails, the main objective of which is to meet guests and get acquainted with them. In informal cocktails, the guests may wear what is suitable for them according to the fashion of the day. The cocktails are normally for the duration of about an hour and a half, though this period may be extended a little, depending on the convenience of the host and the guests. It is evident that conversation and the art of mixing are the soul of a cocktail party. Since cocktail parties are to be small, a person may not be able to invite many friends and acquaintances to one.

The ideal number at a cocktail party may be round about ten, a little more or a little less than that. The guests should bring out their best to mix with one another. However, the guests that are invited are to be mainly regarded as those of the host concerned and other guests normally should not pick up friendship or become intimate with any of them unless they continue to meet in the business world. This rule, however, is not applicable at bigger receptions where friendships may be freely picked up and then cocktail invitations despatched to get to know each other better. Discussions of a general nature are ordinarily the rule at cocktails but there is no harm if the talk moves on to more specified subjects and some sort of semi-business discussions ensue.

It is common courtesy to return a cocktail invitation, that is, give a cocktail invitation to the host who had earlier invited you. But, it is not always necessary that the guests and the hosts should become so intimate as to continue to reciprocate these kind of invitations. Where strong drinks or liquor are served, it is necessary for the guests to know their limits and not get drunk. In this connection a person should know how far he is capable of standing drinks and this limit should not be crossed, for that would cause embarrassment to the host since the party is usually small and compact. Too much boisterousness which may go unnoticed at a reception will not be in place at a cocktail party of a moderate size.

Ceremonial

At ceremonial receptions, the guests and hosts are normally required to observe some form in respect of dress and other matters. At a traditional marriage, the guests in India who are from the bride's side may not partake of the meal or other luxuries of the reception until the bride-groom has arrived with his party, and then too the groom's party has to be attended to first before they may help themselves. It may also rest on the bride's guests to render all possible help and assistance to the marriage-house and, on their own initiative, offer a grand welcome to the groom and his entourage.

The most important etiquette on such occasions is to forget oneself as much as possible and get involved in the ceremony with spirit and good intentions. If in such cases a person gives much importance to small and negligible talk and is too conscious of his own image and prestige, he cannot give himself fully to participation in a ceremonial reception. The guests who come from the bride's side should thus be ready to fill in whatever gaps are there in the reception and they should do all these things without being told and without batting an eyelid, because they must feel apprehensive of the bride's side who may already be in fear of some shortcoming or other in the welcome of the groom's party. Thus such receptions would require the spirit of sacrifice and social work and a person who has a practical bent of mind and a way of mixing with the people would naturally give the best account of himself.

From this point of view, the people in the groom's party in a marriage should also be aware of what is the correct behaviour. They should not take it into their heads to behave like overlords under the impression that since they are accompanying the most important person in the ceremony, they can behave in whatever manner they like. Sometimes their courteous and polite behaviour may bring out the best welcome and service from the other side who may put their hearts into their actions with joy and sincerity.

In like manner, there may be ceremonials like marriage engagements, the religious ceremony of the sacred thread, *mundan* (shaving of the head), and events like these where the guests have to fit in and perform their functions in the manner most desirable.

Hotel Reception

Receptions are mainly held in specially built marriage halls and hotels which are very convenient places for holding these. All the required services like those of the serving personnel etc., are provided by the hotel and there is no running about for the same. One difficulty with a hotel reception is that the party holding the reception has to get acquainted with every nook and corner of the hotel because so many emergencies may arise when the holder of the reception has to come to the help of one who may need such help. This urgency is more to be taken care of because in a hotel, as different from any other building or place which may be hired for the reception, there may not be much opportunity to stay back for a continued survey.

The holder of the reception, therefore, should take all the important people along who are to supervise the reception and afford them full opportunity to have a complete idea of the hotel hall where the reception is to be held. How the food is to be served, where and when, the public conveniences, the entrances and the exits and all other details have to be known by those who will be in charge of the reception. The holders of the reception, that is, the host, the hostess and party should be at the hotel sufficiently before the time fixed for the reception to see to the

155

arrangements, to welcome the guests and to sort out any problem that may arise at the last minute.

Behaviour at a hotel reception is inclined to be a little more on the formal side than if it is held at a private home. This is so because the prestige of the party in relation to the hotel is to be kept in mind. The guests, when they receive the invitation to attend a reception at a hotel have to be particularly careful because apart from the reception party itself, there are rules of the hotel concerned which cannot be violated, and these rules may be more stringent in the better known hotels. Care must also be taken to keep the furniture and fixtures of the hotel intact or the burden of compensation may fall on the host in case of breakages and other mishaps.

House Reception

In a house reception, the important thing is the necessary space and if a house does not have such space which is convenient for the holding of the reception and accommodating all the guests, *pandals* or constructions may be erected adjacent to the house to provide the required space. The proper welcome of the guests is the first etiquette at a house reception. A single smile may be enough to reassure the guest that he is welcome while overlooking to do so may start all the secret grumblings and dissatisfactions. Greetings and acknowledgements are necessary and either the host himself or somebody on his behalf should extend these to the invitees. The inmates of the house should know their responsibilities and should branch out in various directions to meet the guests who have assembled under the decorated canopy. They should never stand together and talk among themselves and look at the guests as outsiders. Each one of the members of the family should take charge of one group at least on his own. The same may be said of the servants or hired hands. They must show mobility and compliance and should know their duties thoroughly. If one has to remonstrate with or take to task one's attendants in front of one's guests, much of the reception-glamour may evaporate.

Even for house receptions, the hour and the duration of the reception may be mentioned on the invitation card, and the guests must keep to this timing or schedule. Because the reception is held at the house and also because the guests happen to be close relatives of the host, it does not give the right to the guests to continue to stay on at the reception far beyond the reception-time. Consideration for the host and the inmates, their fatigue, their inconvenience has to be properly taken note of, and consequently the guests, however friendly they may be with the host, should take themselves off at a reasonable hour unless, of course, there is an express request from the host to the guests to stay on longer. The house stands as a symbol of cordiality of the host for the guests and so in house receptions those in charge should be particularly careful since the blame, if any, for any shortcoming will fall on the host and his party directly.

CHAPTER THIRTEEN

Mannerisms

*E*very man is different from his fellow human beings, and at the same time all men have some characteristics in common. For some it is easy to copy others, while for others their own individualities would assert themselves in spite of their conscious efforts to the contrary. A man has to undergo training for politeness, for manners and for all kinds of good and socially acceptable behaviour. Sometimes this training is received in childhood when he is tender in years, and sometimes he may not be lucky enough to receive such training till quite late in life. Whatever a man inherits naturally is the most impressive trait for which he may be singled out or by which he may be referred to. Sometimes it may be necessary to follow certain actions and movements of others which are representative of some mode of conduct or etiquette. A hand-shake, the manner of standing or sitting, the placing of hands, the way of calling out to somebody in low tones, etc., may be part of certain classes of action. These are not all, however. In the world of manners, there are certain acts or expressions which are on the artificial side, though sometimes they may pass for genuine good manners. These mannerisms are to be avoided at all consts, if a person is desirous of acquiring the best of manners.

Showing-off

This is a kind of behaviour which goes with children or adolescents, but even adults and aged person cannot refrain from it. There is no particular definition of showing-off. A person may try to show off in a variety of circumstances. He may imitate the voice of some person, or the sitting or standing posture of another, or he may talk and laugh like another person, consciously or unconsciously. He may try to pass for a rich man, an educated man, a talented man, a courageous man and so on. Such instances are countless. It has to be admitted, of course, that showing off and passing off for somebody else are not one and the same thing. One may pass off for some type of person once or for a period. When one shows off a particular advantage or achievement, one may flaunt the same in front of others very conspicuously till everybody gets to recognise his good luck or his exalted position.

In such a case, that is, where a person is in possession of something which is really to be praised or which is beyond the capacity of other to get, the showing-off, though falling in the category of bad manners and exhibitionism, is not, however, materially wrong or imporper. A person gets a good job or a new assignment and he gives himself airs. If such behaviour is continued over a reasonable period till the novelty of the situation wears off, there may not be much to be said in criticism. There are, nevertheless, situations when some persons try to show off something which does not properly belong to them, and in such cases the people should be put wise about the futility of such duplicity. If they correct themselves on the advice of others, they may not depart too much from truly correct behaviour.

The training in good behaviour must be given in childhood and as the child grows into youth and subsequently into manhood, the training of the early years may persist, and he may not be tempted to act in a manner which is not at all suited to him, or which is alien to him. It may, therefore, be concluded that showing-off is not only regarded as bad manners but it is also improper and may sometimes border on illegality or the ridiculous. The will to show off may be traced to a person's desire to get prominence and this desire is ventilated in a perverted form because the real worth of the said person which could have been developed has not been properly brought forth.

Affected Style

If showing-off comes from some kind of conceit or peculiar individuality, the assuming of an affected style may be said to be the result of an inner consciousness of some deficiency. When a person feels that he or she is deficient in something, that person may try to cover up this shortcoming by copying the style of another. The affected style nevertheless falls easily into the class of showing-off because it may be taken as an expression of trying to establish oneself and would be akin to the behaviour of an extrovert. A person smokes a cigarette in a different and show off manner, he pronounces certain words differently, he holds his glass or his cup prominently, he wears his dress elaborately in a sophisticated manner. Many of these actions become ingrained

161

in his nature and cannot be remedied due to long use. How far should this somewhat conspicuous, if not unnatural, behavior be tolerated? In reply we may say that not all such manners can be branded as bad manners, like sophistication, or an outstanding taste in dress and decoration, and it may be added that much of this affected behaviour may not look so bad, after all, since it has been ingrained in the general characteristics of the persons concerned.

It cannot be denied that one is prone to copy those whom one loves, admires and adores and ther is no shaking off of this tendency unless one's love for oneself becomes over-prominent to cover the other's image. Other's words and actions may seep into one without knowing and not all of the affectations can be got rid of because these habits may progressively fall off as one progresses on the path of success and acquires his own individual manners. What is, however, advised under the circumstances is that a person should try to strive to establish his own self and to find out the truth about himself. Here he will have to see and analyse what are his individual manners and what he has borrowed from others, which is not a part of his inborn nature. In most cases, a person can easily differentiate between his natural and artificial behaviour if he tries sincerely, or he may rely on the versions and impressions of his friends and relations. If he once takes to artificial behaviour, people may have a poor impression about him because in whatever dreamland he may be for others, it is normally quite easy to know what is real and what is artificial in another's behaviour.

Idiosyncrasies

A person may not take a certain type of food, he may not wear certain types of clothes and adornments, he may not do something on a certain date, he may depend sometimes on certain rituals. All these are the individual's idiosyncrasies and the inclusion of these in the realm of manners is necessary because when stretched to extremes, idiosyncrasies may tantamount to very bad manners. There are all kinds of superstitions associated with these idiosyncrasies and the weaker a person becomes under these influences, the stronger his idiosyncrasies become. This growth of idiosyncrasies in a certain person may be attributed to his secret fear and instability in life and it may not be easy to remove these minor prejudices unless the original fear or instability is also removed. It may be noticed that these things may grow later in life than in youth when a man's possibility for success may be immense.

Youth is thus the period for the removal of idiosyncrasies. This is the time when with a little admonition or conscious effort and introspection the small and big prejudices may be easily eliminated, because in youth they may be prompted by unconscious emulation and nothing else. Idiosyncrasies always stand in the way of a man's complete self-fulfilment, and a man of ambition or idealism has to keep off from all such superfluous burdens. Besides evoking laughter and pity in others where a person blindly follows a superstition or an idiosyncrasy, adherence to these insignificant mannerisms may lead him to cause hurt to another, where he may refuse the light for his smoke because he happens to be the third person at the burning matchstick's end, or he may not take the proffered biscuit because it happens to be the last one on the plate, or he may make no payment because it is a certain day of the week, etc. Apart from the strangeness of the person if we consider the amount of explanations in all these small and simple acts and their possible effects on others, we may realise how important it is to cleanse our minds of such cant and supersitition so that we may be able to lead a normal social life.

Gestures

Every person is endowed with a distinctive personality. His talking, standing and all other movements have to be in tune with this personality. If there is a discord, if his movements are not smooth and natural, he may fail to create an impression on other. Far from that, he may sometimes be ill-mannered and sometimes ludicrous in his behaviour. It is, therefore, one of the main rules of etiquette that one should learn or be taught to move one's hands and feet in a coordinated, agreeable and polite manner. Unnecessary gesticulations may at times prove intolerable or even ludicrous to others, especially in good and gentle company which is used to fine gestures and postures.

When a person is talking to another person, it is not good manners for him to move his hands too much, or raise his shoulders and shrug or toss his head every now and then. Certainly, if a person is not sure of himself, he may not be able to coordinate his movements with his words in an impressive manner. But even otherwise a person may have acquired some habits like touching his moustache or his spectacles or twitching the tip of his nose, or locking his hands together and so on. A well-mannered person will know how to keep his hands to his sides while talking. He may raise his hands, his shoulders or his eyebrows but these gestures should be so timed as not to stand out prominently during his conversation. Sometimes gestures may be so vehement that they may hurt the other party, as when a person bangs his fist on the table or gesticulates like giving a blow, or claps his palms together. These are not civil gestures and if there are ladies present in the group, these are certainly crude and disrespectful. Equally uncivil is loud clapping of hands and slapping another person on the back or some other part of the body without being absolutely sure beforehand that such a gesture will be appreciated by the latter. In fact, a person should not ordinarily touch another person's body unless he is very close to the latter.

Repetition

There are people who go on repeating the same thing over and over again, little realising that this is very annoying to the person who has to listen to all this. If a person repeats somethings for the understanding of another, it would mean that that person is doubting the intelligence of the latter. There are, of course, complex explanations which a person has to repeat for the benefit of the one spoken to. The best thing in the circumstances will be to wait for the other person to put questions, if any. If no question is forthcoming, it may be taken for granted that the listener has understood everything clearly.

There are, however, different situations when repetitions become necessary, as in the case of official work (and the same is true of personal assignments as well). If the doer understands a thing wrongly, the work may be spoiled and losses may be incurred. Even on such occasions, it is more effective to put questions to the person concerned to find out whether the whole thing has been understood perfectly by him.

While repetitions may be expendient in explaining facts and situations to a subordinate, in talking to equals and superiors, repetitions may be considered bad manners. In a working bureaucracy, a superior is supposed to know more and hence to give more than necessary explanations or to repeat things for the understanding of this superior is unnecessary. In speech and writing, repetition is equally ineffective. When the habit of repetition become ingrained in one's nature, one may relish the words that one repeats again and again. There may be persons who may have repeated the same stories at every gathering. Such a person may not be really blamed because he may be doing this unintentionally or unconsciously and if he is at all to be blamed, he is to be blamed for the bad habit he has acquired and cannot get rid of. Only a sustained conscious effort can cure a person of this malady, and a malady it really is since the has got habituated to his repetition and is not fully satisfied unless he says things over and over again.

Smiles and Laughter

Smiling is a charming thing in the sphere of good manners, but if smiles are too frequently given, they may signify the insincerity of the person too obviously. It is also true that difficult situations can be easily got over with the help of timely smiles. However, if a person acquires the habit of smiling all too frequently without a genuine cause, the other side may take offence secretly. This is because smiles which arise without reason, and too profusely all the time, may convey just the opposite of the sense that is purported to be conveyed. Some may interpret these smiles as insolence or sarcasm or taunts. The rule, therefore, is smile by all means but smile moderately and intelligently at the proper time and place.

While smiles which are uncalled for many sometimes border on impudence, laughter at odd moments definitely bespeaks bad manners and ill-breeding or lack of culture. The sound of laughter also bears mention. If a person laughs too loudly or heartily in a group that is not used to such laughter or is not in favour of the same, the laughing person may at once become the object of scorn, ridicule and even ill-feeling for breaking the code of conduct. In business meetings, social gatherings and cultural shows also, a person has to control his urge to laugh loudly and unrestrainedly. There is a fine dividing line between laughter that expresses mirth and the one that expresses scorn, disbelief and so on. A well-behaved person should be acquainted with the art of the right intonations of laughter in different circumstances.

Smiles and laughter fall under the category of mannerisms sometimes because when such gestures are not spontaneous and natural, they may evoke quite the contrary sentiment in others. People can recognise real or artificial smiles and laughter and instead of good effect, much ill-will may be caused unconsciously.

He may be regarded as a fool. It is, therefore, not advisable that a person should have a smiling face and should laugh or smile at every alternate word that he may speak. The smile is reflected in the eyes and real laughter comes from the heart. Where there is lack of these conditions, a smile or a laugh may prove unwelcome and may cause many eyebrows to be raised.

Pretension

Smiles and laughter are one form of pretension but there are other modes too. A person with a sugar-coated tongue may be able to hide his real feelings and may make the other person believe that he is taking a genuine interest in the other's affairs. The notion may find favour with some persons that if a man is not angry or does not show his displeasure in an open way, he is showing good manners. There is no denying that a man of true culture and good manners does not fly into a rage every two seconds. But it is also true that pretending pleasure and suppressing one's anger may be easily detected by another, and then this pretension may include the evil of falsehood and even cheating. In a civilized world nevertheless a person may not express his innermost thoughts all the time and some amount of cover is necessary. As long as this refers to a person's own individuality, there may not be much harm done to the others. But when a person takes action under a pretension, he may motivate something in respect of another. One has to draw the line between good manners and a pretence of good manners while trying to give a different meaning to one's actions.

The most impressive of actions is natural behaviour. If a person has to keep to correct etiquette he must behave naturally and normally in the best possible manner without artificiality. It is said that sometimes a 'no' is more appreciated than an all-the-time 'yes'. Some sort of a mind resistance on the part of someone is not only good but also speaks of his self-respect and restores others' trust in him. A man has to establish himself as well as help others within the ambit of his ability. He has to make his mark in the world and be socially useful. If he resorts to pretence in any form, he might mess up things. His friends may not consider him dependable. His adversaries may deal bigger thrusts to pull him down. His intentions may not be carried across to others. There are circles, however, where pretensions may be appreciated, where intrigues and duplicities are applauded but those may be limited set-ups and may not fall within the purview of common manners where pretensions aggravate a situation. We may safely ignore them as unworthy of our consideration.

CHAPTER FOURTEEN

Interviews

*T*wo persons meet casually and talk in a friendly manner, but when they meet to know each other or to give an account of each other in the best possible light, we have situations that are called interviews. Interviews, therefore, are held to know a person and to test him where necessary for some capability or information. A person may go to an office for an interview for some employment, or he may be interviewed by some social worker with regard to some facts and data for some enquiry. When strangers meet one another, there is some subtle sort of interview that takes place where all the involved parties may try to gather as much information as possible.

Jobs

At interviews for jobs, a person has to give of his best. He has to show his best manners and etiquette. The general disposition in such an interview is sometimes the main factor. The interviewee enters the room where the big bosses are waiting for him. He has to stand before them, wish them and exchange some pleasantries, and then sit down and talk. He has to be calm and composed, for a nervous person may cut a very sorry figure at an interview. Standing to attention, standing good-naturedly, standing officially and standing in a relaxed manner are all different postures. An interviewee has to know the correct posture and sometimes when the interviewers have a good knowledge of the interviewee's way of standing, the latter may be asked to take his seat.

Sitting comes next and the interviewee who has mastered the art of natural and relaxed sitting will make the second good impression. Sitting is sometimes a difficult posture from the interviewee's point of view because while a man is standing he has his physical forces under his control, but when he is sitting his physical forces may be disarrayed. It is better to keep the arms losely at the sides with the hands resting on the thighs. The hands may also rest on the table in front but this has to be done in a manner that will not present any sign of effrontery or slackness or tiredness or indifference.

Word spoken should be clear and unambiguous. Answers should be clear and to the point. The replies should contain some finality and should not contain alternatives. To a question like 'Do you consider games to be important?', the answer should be a clear-cut yes or no, backed, of course, by reasons which may not be given unless demanded. Facial expressions also play a great role in interviews. A person whose expression changes from one moment to another may fail to impress as much as another whose face may remain impassive and expressionless all the time. There should be a free play of expressions and the eyes especially should remain passively intelligent. Handshakes are important and necessary but these should be done only at the initiative of the interviewers. At the end of the interview when the candidate is leaving and standing up, he should wait for a fraction of a second to see whether the interviewers are standing up or not. If they keep sitting, he should bow a little, turn and walk correctly out of the room. He should never extend his hand for a handshake. While leaving the room, he should softy close the door and should never bang it or show that he is in a hurry to leave.

Selling

The meeting with a customer does not amount to a proper interview, strictly speaking, but this may, however, be classified under this type of visit because the customer's response will largely depend on the seller's power to charm and impress him with the former's good behaviour. The questions that a customer naturally is going to ask about the goods he is going to purchase have to be answered fully and to his satisfaction. Only then may sale be assured. But a different kind of attitude is to be maintained in such a case. In an interview for a job the employer or the interviewers. This may not be the case with a customer who may be totally or partially ignorant about his item of purchase. The salesman in such a situation has not only to bring out the good points of the goods that he is going to sell but also he should try his best to convince the customer about their quality without which the customer may not be persuaded to buy the goods and feel that he has got his money's worth.

From the point of goodwill of the concern, it is necessary that every customer may receive expert advice and make his selection for which he may not have regrets latter. It would be the job of a seller to find out or guess a customer's limit of purchase, and his next duty would be to offer the customer a commodity or package of the same which would have maximum utility within price-range. The etiquette of selling in this connection is that the seller's actions must be clear and above board and he should place all his cards on the table, so that the customer may use his reasoning in the desired fashion. It would be absolutely wrong on the part of the seller to try to pass something on to the customer which is unreasonable but since the customer is free to use his intelligence and seek advice before making the purchase, it would be an extra burden on the seller to put up all the weak points of his products. This type of business-reasoning never profits one in the end, and as a form of business as well as of shop etiquette, a customer should be treated with the greatest respect and honesty.

Exploring Contacts

A major part of the salesman's duty is to prepare the background for a sale. Without shrewdness, a salesman's career cannot be made, and it is for the salesman to increase the field of his customers by attracting new customers. However, the salesman's job does not end there and he has to maintain old customers as also restore the confidence of those who had turned away from him earlier. A salesman who loses hope or is discouraged with setbacks is no salesman at all. He has to keep his composure in the face of all types of disappointment. He should never forget to smile nor lose his amiability. There is a sort of amiability which is equivalent to flattery. The salesman has to avoid that, but in its place he should get himself really concerned with the prospective customer.

It is not that a salesman's job ends with the sales talk either at the office or elsewhere. Rather, a salesman's is a wholetime occupation, a twenty-four hour one, plus service to his concern and to his own progressive schemes. A salesman may meet a prospective customer on the street, at the market-place or at some other place off-hand and at once he has to switch on his best manners and goodwill. Such a behaviour should be sincere and natural and should emanate from within and not be shallow or half-hearted. It is also not required for the salesman to press and pester a prospective customer for a sale, but on the contrary, he should realise the difficulties of the customer and should try to solve them with best practical assistance and suggestions. Since a sale is mainly the result of contacts, the salesman has to go on expanding the area of such contacts and for this he has not only to take into view the immediate sale of the product but the possibilities of future sales. He has to spread the knowledge about the good qualities and the localities of its availability and of the things that he is selling and if he is good in paving the way for such sales at a time in some near or distant future, he may be said to have been doing his duties efficiently. Unless, therefore, a salesman takes his profession with the best of intentions and with utmost sincerity and seriousness, he can hardly do well, because aptitude for his job and the nature of his duties will supply him with the relevant props with which he will be able to increase the extent of his influence.

Press

Contacts with the press require a different kind of expertise, because as far as the interview part of the meeting is concerned, the press people may be given all the merits of possessing a sound art. The person meeting the press has only to remember that what he gives out may be printed because it is for that that the press people have been invited, and such a person would be foolish to express his regrets afterwards. There is no denying the fact that the questions that may be put to a person in such an interview will be exploratory in nature. The answers should be straight and to the point. A person at such an interview has to be in control of his senses and his aptitudes because a sudden flaring up on any account would be regarded as a sort of weakness and an inability in him. The questions in such cases are hardly meant to be personal and there is no reason why any person should be so sensitive as to treat them as such. A witty press interview is satifying for the interviewee as well as for the press people. All the questions have their answers and the press interviewee has to find the best-suited answer under the circumstances. The press is for the betterment of the public and the person who is giving a press interview should not forget this nor the benefits and advantages he can bring to his people by meeting people's curiosity. Press interviews, therefore, should be very amiable and comfortable affairs where a liaison between the two sides is given free play to produce common good. Sometimes a press interview is a necessity and the person meeting the press is to be aware of this compulsion, and since the knowledge gathered by the press is to be diffused among the public, the replies to the queriess should be shorn of all adornments or ambiguities. They should be simple, straightforward and clear always.

Dignitary

Noted people sometimes subject themselves to interviews for the good of their people. These men of high positions who may be the doyens or the undisputed leaders in their fields have certain qualities and glamour about them, and it is for the interviewer to respect this glamour and preserve this image. It is unthinkable that an interviewer who approaches a certain expert or a V.I.P. would be asking questions to get enlightened on things. Rather, such an interviewer has to be well-acquainted with the topic that he is going to discuss at the interview and only the most difficult or most essential details and mysteries should be sought to be unravelled by the interviewer. Politeness in the interviewer and proper respect for the personality that is to be interviewed are the needed virtues in him. Moreover, since the interviewer is already aware of the background of the great person, he should help him to open up and if the interviewer leads the line, the great personality may disclose the most important facets of his genius which, normally, he may feel shy to bring out openly.

No disrespect should ever be shown to any dignitary and it would be the duty of the interviewer to keep his own personality in the background. The idea is that the image of the personality under interview has to be enhanced and there should be no occasion for cross-currents of answers and repartees to mar that picture. The interviewer has sincerely to experience this greatness before he can project it properly to others, and it would be good etiquette to identify himself fully with this personality for the time being. It would be bad manners to give imprtance to the questions and not to their answers.

Equals

Interviews between two equals are generally in the nature of a visit which is made by one person to another and vice versa. It is easy to deal with such a situation when the persons concerned know of dealings with both superiors and subordinates. If two masters meet, naturally they would know how to treat each other and what to say and what to avoid. The difficulty may arise when two persons though equal in status have not much experience of their rights and duties so as to make the other party feel at home. t goes without saying that when two equals meet, ordinary ormalities of courtesy may be dispensed with and the conversation, if necessary, may proceed along intimate terms. The welcome accorded to each other has to be very cordial and besides the handshake, etc., ther may be other close contacts like even embracing, holding each other and so on. There is no particular mode of such a welcome and it would depend on the mood, usual practice and inclinations of the two equals.

Among equals the questions that are exchanged pertain to a different character, and very probing questions may or may not be put, depending on the relationship. However, sometimes when the relationship is close, there is no end to the intimacies in enquiries that they may indulge in. They may behave like boys, young men or old men as and when they feel the same convenient. It would, therefore, be natural for equals to crack jokes and speak in a manner that is informal. Neither of the equals should take offence at this and they should laugh away and give themselves up to the pleasure of the meeting. When we speak of equals, we mean that two or more persons are equals not only in point of present position or status but that they also have the same background or, alternatively, have acquired enough knowledge of a similar background required for such a position or status. If there is any discrepancy in respect of any inherent quality, the equality may not be perfect and equal manner or behaviour may be misunderstood by one side or another.

Unequals

When two persons know they are unequal in position or background, they may be at peace when in discourse with each other because each may know how to behave with the other and there may be no grievance or grumbling on either side. Certainly there is the question of humanity and on the basis of the fact that all persons are human beings, there should be no quesiton of any difference in behaviour. In the practical world, however, there may be many gradations and the same person may be superior to one and subordinate to another. From this practical aspect, it is necessary that two such unequal persons may meet and if they are aware of their rights and duties, there may be no hitch and the relationship or contact may go on smoothly. While meeting

179

socially, not officially, it is for the superior to come down and not for the subordiante to comp up.

It would be wrong for a superior to show official aloofness, but he has to behave normally taking interest in the person who may happen to be placed below him. It is he who should ask about all the problems and provide all the moral assistance and let the other person feel secure and at ease. For the person who happens to be lower in position, it may appear to be awkward or unnatural if he tries to compete with others who are his superiors, at the same time remembering that beyond the official relationship in the outside social world, being human counts a great deal and he should not feel inferior even if his position is lower. If such a man can bring to the forefront all his other good qualities, he will earn his place in society outside the official sphere; only he has to know the line demarcating politeness from flattery. and smartness from insolence.

CHAPTER FIFTEEN

Travel

*T*ravelling apart from visual and other experiences, imparts training to a person as to how he should cope with diverse and different situations with which he may not have much connection in his daily life. Firstly, there is the physical exertion involved in travel that makes a man alert to face realities. Even if the travel or tour schedule is perfectly chalked out, there may always arise contingencies which require solutions on the spot. Repeated encounters, like unwanted or unforeseen situations during the period a person is travelling, may make him strong enough to be immune to all such incidents.

General

The moment a person leaves his home and is on the move, he is on his own. It is only his self-confidence on which he may rely during his journey. He has to meet different kinds of people even if he is a quiet type and in the course of his dealings with porters, railway or airport staff, hotel personnel, taxi-drivers and so on, he learns how to tackle people and project his own personality on them. This type of personality, however, he can acquire only as and when he gathers experience. It goes without saying that there may always be a few first times when he may find himself duped or in an impossible position. Since such an experience cannot be emulated or acquired vicariously, a person travelling for the first time has to throw himself at the mercy of a whole lot of persons without whose assistance he cannot successfully complete his journey.

Irrespective of the etiquette and manners that a person may like to show, he has to follow the simple rule of behavng strongly with the strong and gently with the weak. If he does not have the courage to give back what he takes, he may have to finish his travels with constant fear and insecurity. But there are no grounds for becoming rude and rough, and the friends that a person makes through gentleness and good behaviour may be of immense help to him during his journey. The use of common sense is essential, and with it an eye for the genuine and the good. If he can at once guess through conversation who is a good man out to help him and who is not, he may be able to save or get over much of the trouble that may come his way. Just as he is to be self-protecting in case of aggression or impediments, so also he has to be helpful and sincere when somebody needs his help. The idea is to keep an open mind, take advice and make contacts as far as possible.

Public Dealings

This may refer to the etiquette of those who are in charge of travels and tours. The tourist or traveller is generally in search of good advice and it is the public relations people at the airports, at the railway stations, at the travel agents, offices to whom the tourist has to turn. Sometimes the tourist is experienced and sometimes he is not and it is the responsibility of all these people who are providing service to the public to do so with the greatest of consideration and care. A man at the enquiry counter may have to answer the same questions daily and all the time and yet each time it is new for somebody who may have come distractedly to that counter. If the public relations man realises this and is also sympathetic with the predicaments of those who are in need of advice, correctly and quickly, he may never turn mechnical at his job but may give answers with renewed energy every time.

It is true that the traveller should show patience and fortitude and should not get upset at the smallest inconvenience. Mistakes are sure to occur on both sides but these can be sorted out and solved with a cool head and mature understanding than with mistrust and misbehaviour. So the traveller has to be polite to the officials who may be handling his affairs and with gentleness and tact, a better performance may be extracted than with an aggressive attitude of complaint. Like all public relations men, these men who man the counters and the key-points in travel enhance the prestige of the organisation that they work for and if it happens to be the Government, the foreign tourist who gets advice and help from a railway guard, a porter or taxi-driver will go back with happy memories of this country. It is, of course, required that such public relations posts are given to those alone who are experienced and new personnel may be positioned only after proper training and a period of apprenticeship.

Fellow-Travellers

Fellow-travellers may have to face the same difficulties, the same obstacles, the same problems. To help each other when both are travellers is but natural and the new traveller learn a great deal from the old and experienced one. However, even if the obstructions faced by the different travellers may be the same, the inclinations and reactions of the travellers may be different and so the experienced traveller may advise and guide, but should not particularly compel the other traveller to take a certain course of action. In accommodation, in food, city tours, the preferences of the travellers may be different and if one traveller has to move with his fellow-travellers involuntarily, the charm of travel may be lost to him. There is a line of individuality in such behaviour and no self-respecting traveller may proceed with friendship beyond the limit to which the other traveller is willing to go. This is not to be taken as a personal hurt but a natural act, for a tourist and a fellow-tourist have to catch this right mood.

In travels the novelty may lie in most cases in exploraiton on one's own and not under someone's guidance. Those who make use of the services of a guide may do so for some sort of protection or otherwise, but there may be other fellow-tourists who may dislike very much the idea of lugging a guide along. It is common courtesy that one fellow should stand by another in the face of some trouble, whether the same is faced jointly or singly by one of the fellow-travellers. This form of etiquette should not be given up even if the travellers concerned do not have much in common. It is also politeness to bid one another goodbye before parting and to enquire if the fellow-traveller needs any help or advice. Normally, of course, personal matters are not discussed unless one thing may lead to another and the travellers may become friendly. Also, the same intimacy of joint travel cannot ordinarily be referred to or depended upon in future contacts, if any.

Transporters

They are an essential part of any travel, and even if one carries one's suitcase oneself, there are vehicles that one has to hire and on whose honesty one has to depend. It may be unlikely that a tourist has been to the same city twice to know the behaviour-pattern of the transport personnel, and so some amount of natural grit and general courage may be called for. A strong and steady attitude and general alertness may depend more on one's practical sense and nature than on any other source.

Cool courage and unruffled calmness may sometimes be more effective, and even if the worst comes to the worst, one should never lose one's head but should hold one's ground with determination and strength. In all such encounters, weakness in a person is disagreeable to the other person who is to deal with the former.

A traveller who is nervous and panicky from the first and shows his suspicion openly makes it difficult for another to help him and some kind of a row is a possible natural consequence. If, on the other hand, such a person is confident and amiable and engages the other man in pleasant conversation, being alert and observant at the same time, some sort of liaison or rapport may be established between the traveller and the transporter, and the latter may provide better service to the former. Some travellers may treat the driver or the transporter very kindly and in a friendly way. He may treat the latter to drinks and even lunch and dinner that he may be having for himself. Such behaviour, no doubt, endears the traveller to the transporter and in such a cordial relationship, the chances of misunderstanding are very few. It is, therefore, throught love and friendship that the foreign or any tourist has to win the transporter over to his side because it is naturally advisable to avoid an unpleasant situation or a scene. Certainly, in the face of inevitable evil, the traveller has to put his foot down and take a firm stand, come what may.

Others

There may be a whole lot of other people of undefinable category with whom the traveller has to deal. They may be the agents of a product or agency, the sellerss of goods, private guides and other persons. There may also be freelancers or interviewers who may be contacting travellers for some information or other. Then ther are coolies, gatekeepers, hotel and room attendants. If the traveller is alone, he may have nobody to depend upon unless he can requisition the assistance of the hotel authorities or any other authority which may be under obligation to help the tourists. The traveller has to acquire a mature character showing enough confidence during the course of his journey. If he fails in this objective and remains immature and dependent even at the end of all his travels, there may be nothing that may be said in his favour. This confidence should become ingrained in him and he should not try to show off or prove his superiority nor should he sound over-confident or become talkative or too intimate.

It is his own reasoning that the traveller has to depend on ultimately and he may keep this reasoning clear if he adopts the middle course and behaves correctly. He has to maintain a firm but civil tone, and has to examine every proposition by giving a careful thought before accepting it. One thing which any tourist with good judgement should avoid is an invitation from a stranger for stay, food arrangements or conducted tours, etc. In this respect, it would be better for him to move with the crowd than to do something totally on his own. The way of the majority may not be outstanding but it may be the average way replete with all comforts and considerations that may be expected ordinarily. To get to something outstanding, the traveller would do well to get the help of some person or person in whose bonafides he has trust. In the matter of tipping also, travellers have to be somewhat cautious and if they tip more or if they do the contrary, both these things may go against them. It is, therefore, necessary for a traveller to get and study a travel guide or get complete information, etc., about the place from some reliable source before dealing with or engaging the services of others in a new place.

be indifferent, and they may also be totally opposed to each other. The liaison work will have to take in its stride all these possibilities and practical situations and after a thorough analysis of the same, stresses and strains will have to be ironed out and mutual appreciation and inclinations have to be enhanced and sharpened.

In the face of the existing goodwill, the liaison-man may have little more to do than be present at the opportune moments to remind and redouble the good feelings that are already there between them.

When the situation is the other way round, the liaison work may be charged with a far greater responsibility. In uch a situation, the liaison worker has to proceed firmly and with discretion and has to project the right image of the side that he is representing. Sometimes when the feelings between the two parties are not so good owing to some previous misunderstanding, the person negotiating at the moment has to use all his charm and best etiquette. He has to be patient with the opposite party and be able to view the whole situation from their side and thus remove all the grievances that this side may be harbouring. After such a neutralisation of the accumulated prejudices, the work at hand of straightening out the differences may proceed. A pliable character and good-natured disposition are assest on which liaison-men should bank and they should never allow their feelings of irritation to get the better of them.

getting may be genuine and inspired by a deep understanding. The well-behaved person will naturally try to avoid all unpleasant incidents not because he is afraid to face or live upto them but because such things destroy, forever, the style and beauty of living which once disrupted may not be capable of being captured again. This feeling for form and correct attitude in life can be made to reflect in others whom the well-mannered man may meet. Even if these others are used to the crude ways of life, a well-mannered person can quite easily work on their inner human feelings to produce harmonious music which is the guiding principle of living side by side with accord.

Liaison

There is the way of doing things in one's own way. There is also the way of doing things with others. In the latter case the actions of two or more persons can be well-timed and coordinated if there is proper understanding in all persons concerned. A great part of the work-a-day world is related to the conveying of one's intention and its full import to another whose cooperation is needed. The presentation of one's proposal to the other party has to be done through the proper channel and the manners that are to be observed in such business or the conveying of intentions from one party to another is the essence of the art of liaison. Two parties are brought close to each other though they may be differently disposed towards each other. They may be eager to meet and negotiate; they may not be so eager, that is, they may

*T*here is beauty and grace in good manners and these are appreciated almost everywhere. What is particularly satisfying to a person who possesses good manners and correct etiquette is his self-confidence. He will seldom be ruffled by others. He is the master of the situation in which he may find himself. The odds of his encounters do not frighten him. He also has an advantage over others because it may be quite possible that people will have to give him, even grudgingly, precedence and follow his example. In most cases, however, he may generate in others enough respect and admiration, and possibly, also, love, and give him, literally, the right of way in nearly all situations.

The satisfaction that is caused by a well-behaved person belongs not only to the person himself but the other party or parties with whom the former may come in contact. Satisfaction is pleasure and relief in knowing that the *status quo* of any given situation would be maintained without express directions and interventions. From this relief, other natural feelings like mutual appreciation and fellow-feeling grow and it is for this that many a gentleman-crook wins the hearts of the people he contacts with the help of good behaviour, politness and civility. Such incidents happen because the person concerned may rouse the feeling of gratitude in others and so the help or the trust that he may be

Conclusion